Galaxy of Funny Gags, Puns, Quips and Putdowns

Also by the Author

5,000 One and Two Liners for Any and
   Every Occasion

Encyclopedia of Ad-Libs, Crazy Jokes, Insults
   and Wisecracks

Galaxy of Funny Gags, Puns, Quips and Putdowns

Leopold Fechtner

Parker Publishing Company, Inc.

West Nyack, New York

©1980 by

PARKER PUBLISHING COMPANY, INC.

West Nyack, New York

Library of Congress Cataloging in Publication Data

Fechtner, Leopold,
  Galaxy of funny gags, puns, quips and putdowns.

  1. Public speaking—Handbooks, manuals, etc.
2. American wit and humor.   I.   Title.
PN4193.I5F4   818'.5'407   79-18414
ISBN 0-13-346056-8

Printed in the United States of America

This book is dedicated to my lovely wife, Fini.
who has been my constant inspiration,
and whose love and devotion
helped me a great deal
in preparing this
humor book.

How You Can Use This Book for Successful Writing and Entertaining

Humor has always been a fundamental ingredient in speaking, writing and performing. It adds spice to any talk, and properly used, will amuse any audience, will emphasize a certain point, and will pep up the conversation at any party.

This book is a powerful tool for anyone who has to speak, perform, entertain or write and who needs witty sayings and punchy quips to flavor a presentation.

This assembly of new and fresh funny material has never before been compiled in book form.

Each joke needs some personal identification, but a good speaker or writer will never use any material that could offend or irritate a person or a group of people. Therefore, not to embarrass or insult anybody in the audience, it is advisable to joke about yourself, about members of your family or about your friends.

Compiled here is mostly material of this kind, filling a void in the large selection of available humor books. This lively collection of thousands of side-splitting gags, personalized jokes, clever puns and hilarious one-liners provides you with a basic platform to create humorous talks, amusing speeches and sparkling conversations.

These gags will spice up any speech, will inspire and stimulate audiences and are guaranteed to liven up every conversation. All these funny lines are brief, sharp, to the point and are also ideal for use whenever you're making a speech on a serious subject and want to lead into it very gracefully.

Whether the occasion is light or serious, if you include a little humor you will get the full attention of your audience and make your speech warmer, more human and delightfully funny.

A funny line will help put any audience at ease and will help you to overcome any embarrassing moments.

This collection of gags and puns will create a lot of laughter. With a little twist or switch these gags can be applied to any other person in general and can be used to fit any situation or occasion.

To make people smile is an art that can be easily mastered by anyone by using the right gag at the right time.

Holding the attention of an audience is always a serious concern, but by injecting some humorous lines into your lecture or speech, you will capture and hold attention and will be recognized as an interesting and witty speaker.

Experienced speakers will not face an audience unprepared. They know and understand how to organize a speech, where and how to add some funny lines and how to enrich a speech with an unexpected joke.

These especially selected gags are the best tools to make any speech fascinating, colorful and humorous. They will also improve your speech and make any conversation sparkle.

This book is a must for everyone who writes, speaks or lectures. By putting some funny lines into your speeches you will keep your listeners alert, amused, interested and smiling.

Whether you are a speaker, a writer, a performer or someone who has to stand up occasionally and make a speech, give a talk or lecture, this book will help you to "humorize" even your daily conversation. Just include some of these funny lines and you will harvest laughter and be admired for your fine sense of humor.

Use this material tactfully, tastefully and effectively to amuse yourself or any audience on <u>any</u> occasion. Now you can liven up a social gathering with well-timed laughter and <u>hold</u> the guests spellbound.

Leopold Fechtner

Contents

Galaxy of Funny Gags, Puns, Quips and Putdowns

1

My
Crazy
Friend

He accidentally fell through a harp and now he's in the hospital in rooms 34, 35 and 36.

He acquired a large vocabulary—he got married.

He always carries extra matches around to find the fuse box just in case his girl's light goes out.

He always dresses fit to kill, but nobody's had the nerve yet.

He always drives his car in the summer with all windows closed to make believe his car is air-conditioned.

He always eats alphabet soup so he can read while eating.

He always stands before the mirror with his eyes closed so he can see how he looks when he is asleep.

He always wears a plaid suit to keep a check on his stomach.

He bought a car for three people. One drives and two push.

He bought a trouble-free car. The trouble came free with the car.

He bought some cheap shirts and changed his name to fit the monogram.

He broke his drum just to see what made all that noise.

He calls his boat 'Canasta' because it has two decks.

He can't help being stupid. He's got cavities in his wisdom teeth.

He changed his name to Hilton so it would be the same as the name on his towels.

He composes music in bed. He calls it sheet music.

He couldn't carry a tune if it had a handle.

He crossed:

A bee with a lightning bug and got a bee that can work at night.

A black widow spider with a horse. He doesn't know what he's got, but if it ever bites him he can ride to the doctor.

A bowl of alphabet soup with flour and got monogrammed pancakes.

A bridge with a car and got on the other side.

A cactus with an orange and got spiked orange juice.

A camel with a greyhound and got a camel that seats 40 people.

A chicken with a bowling ball. Now the eggs come rolling along.

A commuter train with prune juice and got a train that runs regularly.

A cow with a mule and got milk with a kick to it.

A cow with a zebra and got striped milk.

MY CRAZY FRIEND

A cow with an octopus and got a do-it-yourself dairy.

A dog with a hen and got poached eggs.

A dog with a pig and got a pet that fetches garbage.

A dog with a zebra and got striped sausages.

A duck with a steamroller and got pressed duck.

A flea with a rabbit and got a bug's bunny.

A highway with a bicycle and got killed.

A jellyfish with an electric eel and got current jelly.

A kangaroo with a cow and got an animal that gives milk and carries its own bucket.

A kangaroo with a dog and got a pooch with a pouch.

A kangaroo with a saddle horse and now he can ride inside when it rains.

A kangaroo with a sheep and got a woolly jumper.

A mink with a gorilla and got a nice coat—only the sleeves are too long.

A mink with a kangaroo and got a mink coat with pockets.

A mink with an octopus and got a fur coat with eight sleeves.

A moth with a glowworm and got moths that can fly in dark closets.

A movie with a swimming pool and got a dive-in movie.

A Mexican jumping bean with pancake batter and got self-flopping pancakes.

A parakeet with a centipede and got a walkie-talkie.

A parakeet with a tiger. He doesn't know what he's got, but when it talks, you listen.

A parrot with a hen and got a hen that tells him every time she lays an egg.

A parrot with a hyena so it could tell the world what it's laughing about.

A pig with an octopus and got a football that can throw itself.

A pigeon with a canary and got a bird that sings the message.

A pigeon with a parrot and got a pigeon that can ask directions in case it gets lost.

A pigeon with a woodpecker. Now the pigeon can knock on the door when delivering the message.

A porcupine with a gorilla. Whatever he got, it always gets a seat on the subway.

A potato with a sponge. It tastes terrible, but holds a lot of gravy.

A potato with an onion and got potatoes with watery eyes.

A rabbit with a piece of lead and got a repeating pencil.

A raccoon with a skunk and got a dirty look from the raccoon.

A record player with an air-conditioner and got something for people who like to play it cool.

A sheep with a chocolate bar and got a Hershey Baa.

A silkworm with a garter snake and got silk garters.

A tailor with a post office and got a zipper code.

A turkey with a centipede so everybody could have a drumstick.

A turkey with a kangaroo and got the first turkey you can stuff from the inside.

A woodpecker with a ballpoint pen and got a woodpecker with a retractable beak.

A wristwatch with helium and now he can see time fly.

An asparagus with mustard and got a hot tip.

An electric blanket with a toaster and now he pops out of bed.

An electric blanket with his pajamas and now he wakes up with barbecued ribs.

An electric eel with a sponge and got a shock absorber.

An elephant with a chicken and got a trunkful of eggs.

An elephant with a cow and got four quarts of peanut butter.

An elephant with a parakeet and got an animal that never forgets and tells everything it remembers.

An elephant with a parrot and got a big bird that eats peanuts.

An intersection with a convertible and got a blonde.

An octopus with a bale of straw and got a broom with eight handles.

An onion with garlic and got very lonesome.

He buys a large car when he can finally afford a small one.

He cut off his arms so he could wear a sleeveless sweater.

He cut off his fingers so he could write shorthand.

He cut off his hands so he could play piano by ear.

He couldn't find a parking place for his car so he bought one that was already parked.

He dates only retired school teachers because they have no class and no principals.

He didn't come from a big family. He was sent.

He died a natural death. He was hit by a car.

He discovered a cure for amnesia, but forgot what it was.

He discovered a wonderful way to avoid taxes. He doesn't work.

He does a terrific cha-cha—no matter what the band plays.

He does other things besides drink. He hiccups.

He doesn't brand his cattle. He is so rich, he engraves them.

He doesn't drink to be sociable. He drinks to get drunk.

He doesn't enjoy drinking, but it gives him something to do.

He doesn't mind girls who kiss and tell. At his age he needs all the advertising he can get.

He doesn't really drink. He just gargles with whiskey and sometimes it slips.

He doesn't trust anybody. He even makes his shadow walk in front of him.

He doesn't worry about talking in his sleep. His wife and girlfriend have the same name.

He drank eight Cokes and burped 7-Up.

He drank some cleaning fluid to get rid of the spots in front of his eyes.

He drinks only to forget, but the only thing he forgets is when to stop.

He drinks so much beer that when he eats pretzels you can hear them splash.

He drowned in his sleep. The bed spread, the pillow slipped and he fell into the spring.

He fed his cow batteries so he could blow her horn.

He gets seasick watering the lawn.

He gets two vacations a year—when his son goes to college and when his wife goes to Florida.

He goes to a drive-in movie on a one-seat motorcycle.

He goes to the drive-in movie with a rented double-decker bus. He likes to sit in the balcony.

He got a job as a street peddler, but he went broke. Nobody wanted to buy a street.

He got a job in a laundry because he had a good line.

He got a medal for bravery on the beach. Rescued a girl from a lifeguard.

He got an oval hairbrush, but who wants to brush oval hair?

He got off the bus backwards because he heard they were going to grab his seat.

He got three tickets for jaywalking. One more and they take away his shoes.

He grew up, but his brain didn't.

He had a bad accident. He tried to fly his plane through a tunnel without checking the time schedule.

He had a bad allergy. He was allergic to work.

He had a crush on a lady in the balcony, but she brushed him off.

He had a peach of a secretary until his wife canned her.

He had a three-piece combo: An organ, a cup and a monkey.

He had all his romances carried off without a hitch.

He had an unfortunate accident in his childhood. He was born.

He had bad eyesight until he was eight. Then he got a haircut.

He had bad luck all his life, but when they dug his grave they struck oil.

He had his head examined, but they couldn't find anything.

He had many chances to get married, but never took a chance.

He had no coins to toss into the fountain so he tossed in a check instead.

He had such a long face, the barber charged him twice for shaving.

He had the manners of a gentleman. I knew they didn't belong to him.

He had to give up drinking for his wife and kidneys.

He has a brain, but it hasn't reached his head yet.

He has a concrete mind. All mixed up and permanently set.

He has a cool head and cold feet.

He has a drinking problem. He will never spend money on it.

He has a good head on his shoulders and it's a different one every night.

He has a leading part in the theater. He's a head usher.

He has a lean look. Every time I see him he's leaning on something.

He has a lot of funny lines—too bad they are all in his face.

He has a mechanical mind, but he keeps forgetting to wind it up.

He has a mechanical mind. Too bad some of the screws are missing.

MY CRAZY FRIEND

He has a new car with chrome all over the hood and chrome all over the trunk. It's the chromiest car I have ever seen.

He has a personality that lights up a room—when he walks out.

He has a photographic mind. Too bad it never developed.

He has a single thought—staying that way.

He has a very absorbing job. He makes blotters.

He has an automobile thirst and a wheelbarrow income.

He has an even temper—always grouchy.

He has an impediment in his speech—his wife.

He has an iron constitution. Every time he goes swimming he comes home rusty.

He has appeared on radio, TV, stage and screen. There's no way to escape him.

He has been drinking for three days because his wife left him. That's a long time for celebrating.

He has been seen everywhere with women except at the altar.

He has faults he doesn't even know about.

He has feet so big that he has to put his pants on over his head.

He has leaned on so many bars that his clothes have padded elbows.

He has liquid assets. He keeps his money in his water bed.

He has made up his mind that he can't make up his mind.

He has muscles like potatoes in his arms—mashed potatoes!

He has music in his soul—even his shoes squeak.

He has never come up with anything definite that a girl can put on her finger.

He has never weakened during a weekend.

He has no buttons on his shirt, but no hand in his pocket either.

He has no children to speak of.

He has no one to blame for his mistakes but himself.

He has no one to share his troubles. Also, he very rarely has troubles.

He has no ties except those that need pressing.

He has one car, two suits, three girlfriends and four parking tickets.

He has Pullman teeth—one upper and one lower.

He has real trouble. His wife and his TV set are not working.

He has so many books in his house that every time I enter I have to show my library card.

He has so many wrinkles on his forehead that he has to screw on his hat.

He has spent a pretty penny on girls, but that's about all he's spent.

He has such a low mind he wears his socks to bed to keep his neck warm.

He has such bad handwriting, I don't know if he can spell or not.

He has such big feet they use him to stamp out forest fires.

He has taken advantage of the fact that marriage is not compulsory.

He has teeth like the Ten Commandments—all broken.

He has the craziest hobby. All day long he sits in the corner and collects dust.

MY CRAZY FRIEND

He has the whole closet for himself.

He has to make only one breakfast.

He has to wash his own back.

He has trouble with his hair. It's waving goodbye.

He has troubles. Men don't trust him too far and girls don't trust him too near.

He has two weeks to live. After that his wife will be back from her vacation.

He has water on his brain and liquor on his mind.

He hasn't an enemy in the world, but all his friends hate him.

He hasn't found a girl worth giving up his phone for.

He hasn't slept for days. It's a good thing he sleeps at night.

He heard that turtles live two hundred years so he bought one to find out if it was true.

He hired an upstairs maid and I'm worried. He lives in a hotel room.

He stopped complaining about his wife's cooking after she hit him with the Bromo-Seltzer.

He will all but break his neck to save ten minutes that he will waste anyway.

He will always lose weight when his wife is dieting.

He will always talk baseball in his office and will always talk business on the golf course.

He will cross the ocean to fight for his country, but won't cross the street to vote in an election.

He will eat French toast, Portuguese sardines, Russian dressing, Swiss chocolate, but not American cheese.

He will go anywhere, but not to the rear of the bus.

He will jog ten minutes for exercise and then take the elevator up to the second floor.

He will jump traffic lights to save seconds, then wait for hours for the first tee.

He will oil the lawn mower for his wife every Saturday morning before he goes out to play golf.

He will pay 25 cents to park his car so he won't be fined $2 while spending 15 cents for a 10-cent cup of coffee.

He will spend half a day looking for his vitamin pill, which should make him live longer; then he drives 90 miles an hour on wet pavement to make up for lost time.

He will work hard on a farm, so he can move to the city, where he can make money, so he can retire on a farm.

He works himself to death so he can buy labor-saving devices.

He works himself to death so he can live comfortably.

He would be a rich man if he had a million dollars.

He would buy a new car if he could afford it.

He would change his job if he could find a better one.

He would like to call the Better Business Bureau for a better business.

He invented:

A bald wig for people who want to be bald.

A barstool with seat belts for shaky drinkers.

A bathtub without a plug for people who always take showers.

A battery-operated fork that automatically winds spaghetti.

A battery-operated Q-tip.

A battery-operated toothpick for lazy people.

A beer glass with a magnifying bottom for watching television.

MY CRAZY FRIEND

A black bulb for people who like to sit in the dark.

A bladeless knife without a handle for people who only use spoons.

A blindfold for people who don't want to watch television.

A book without pages for people who can't read.

A breadless sandwich for people who can't eat bread.

A broom-umbrella for people who sweep floors in houses with leaky roofs.

A cake made from yeast and shoe polish for people who like to rise and shine.

A candy bar stuffed with lettuce for people who are on a diet.

A car that would run on water. But at the final test, it sank.

A car without wheels for people who don't go any-place.

A car without a horn for people who don't give a hoot.

A cellophane book that you can read in a restaurant while watching your hat and coat.

A cellophane mattress. Now you don't have to jump out of bed to find out who is underneath.

A cellophane newspaper for wives who'd like to see their husbands at breakfast.

A cigarette containing Mexican jumping beans. It flicks its own ashes.

A cigarette with a cough drop filter.

A cigarette with earplugs for people who don't want to hear why they shouldn't smoke.

A clock without numerals for people who don't care what time it is.

A cocktail shaker with a built-in fire extinguisher. When you get lit you can put yourself out.

A coffee cup with a hole on the bottom. Saves you the trouble of spilling the coffee into the saucer.

A collapsible car jack.

A comb with two teeth for people who wear toupees.

A compass for grapefruits. It tells which way the juice will squirt.

A contact lens for nearsighted electric eyes.

A cure for which there's no disease.

A dandruff that prevents falling Vaseline.

A double-decker bathtub for people who like to sing duets.

A double-pipe for smoking two kinds of tobacco at the same time.

A drip-dry necktie. If you drip gravy on it, it dries in a second.

A dull pencil called 'Neversharp.'

A feather-weight paperweight.

A flameproof match.

A foghorn sharpener for captains who are hard of hearing.

A fountain pen with tweed ink that leaks the color of your suit.

A frozen band-aid for cold cuts.

A goldfish bowl with postcards around it to make the goldfish believe it is going somewhere.

A hot dog 40 feet long. It takes care of a whole row at the circus.

A jacket with buttons in front and back so nobody can tell whether you are coming or going.

A knitted saltshaker cover.

A lightless cigarette lighter for people who stopped smoking.

A lockless key for a keyless lock.

A machine that takes a car apart in five seconds. It's called a locomotive.

A marshmallow cola. It's really a soft drink.

A mattress soaked in ether for people who have trouble falling asleep.

A mattress stuffed with bowling balls so you can roll right out of bed.

A milk carton that opens just as easily as a beer can.

A mixture of corn flakes and toothpaste so people can eat and brush their teeth at the same time.

A new cure for seasickness. It's called a tight collar.

A new detergent. It makes your hands shiny and your dishes soft.

A new drug that cures penicillin.

A new kind of television without a screen. It's called 'Radio.'

A new pen. Fill it with water and it writes under ink.

A new pen that writes under sand—for the French Foreign Legion.

A new pen with meatball points. It writes under gravy.

A new refrigerator with peepholes for people who want to see the light go out.

A new soap. It doesn't clean, it doesn't lather, it doesn't bubble, it's just company in the tub.

A new soap that leaves your wash rough and red, but your hands come out whiter than new.

MY CRAZY FRIEND

A new type of anchovy paste to mend broken anchovies.

A new type of car with a built-in map-refolder.

A new type of skis. After a spill they turn into crutches.

A newspaper that sticks to the ceiling for people who like to read while gargling.

A noiseless firecracker for people who hate noise.

A pair of gloves with phosphorescent thumbs for hitchhiking in the dark.

A pair of reversible roller skates for backward people.

A parachute that opens on impact.

A pencil with erasers on both ends for people who make nothing but mistakes.

A perforated umbrella.

A perfume called 'Mother-in-law.' It smells like trouble.

A perfume that drives women crazy. It smells like money.

A phone without a dial for people who don't make any calls.

A piano with stationary keys for people who would rather play the violin.

A plastic sheet of music for people who like to sing in the shower.

A portable cuckoo clock.

A portable electric can opener for portable electric cans.

A portable electric blanket for people who walk in their sleep.

A product that's guaranteed to put you to sleep—home movies.

A reading lamp without a bulb for people who can't read.

A revolving goldfish bowl for goldfish who can't swim.

A ripcord for pajamas. Now you can bail out of bed.

A road map for people who walk in their sleep.

A rocking chair with seat belts.

A round mailbox for circular letters.

A saltshaker without holes for people who don't use salt.

A shoehorn for horseshoes.

A silent piano for people who don't like music.

A smokeless tobacco. You chew it.

A snow melting device. It's called 'Sunshine.'

A soup spoon with a bell attached to cover the noise.

A special hair cream. It doesn't grow hair, but it shrinks your head to fit the hair you've got.

A sprinkling can without a bottom for people who have artificial flowers.

A square bathtub so you won't get a ring.

A stepladder without steps for washing windows in the cellar.

A sundial that works on Daylight Savings Time.

A teaspoon with a bent handle so people won't hurt their eyes when they drink.

A telephone that only rings when you are awake.

A toaster with knives on each side to scrape the toast as it pops up.

MY CRAZY FRIEND

A toothbrush with a little whip attached for people who want to beat their gums.

A toothless comb for baldheaded people.

A toothpaste with food particles in it for people who get hungry while brushing.

A toothpaste with onion in it for people who are anti-social.

A two-legged card table for people who live in small houses.

A two-legged tripod for very small cameras.

A vertical bed for people who like to sleep standing up.

A waterproof match for giving a hot foot on rainy days.

A weightless paperweight for weak people.

A wig with built-in curlers for women who want to shop in supermarkets.

A windshield that won't hold a parking ticket.

A windshield wiper for eyeglasses.

A wristwatch without a wristband for people who keep it in the drawer.

A wood-burning microwave oven.

An alarm clock for actors. It doesn't ring. It applauds.

An alarm clock that doesn't ring for people who don't have jobs.

An alarm clock with half a bell to wake only one person in the room.

An alarm clock without a bell for people who like to sleep late.

An artificial false tooth.

An elastic seat belt for people who eat while driving.

An electric sundial to check the time by night.

An imitation Cadillac.

An umbrella for dogs so they can go out on rainy nights.

An unsinkable submarine.

An upside down lighthouse for skin divers.

Artificial wood for artificial fireplaces.

Collapsible chairs.

Colored sleeping pills for people who like to dream in technicolor.

Contact lenses with horn rims.

Dogfood that tastes like a postman's leg.

Kiss-proof lipstick. It's made from Limburger cheese, onions and garlic.

Portable television sets that you have to wind up hourly.

Rubber books for people who like to read in the shower.

Rubber money for people who want to stretch their dollars.

Something that will keep all bills down—a heavy paperweight.

Sunglasses for electric eyes.

The most powerful glue, but nobody can open the bottle.

Unbreakable glass for fire alarm boxes.

He is a born loser:

He bought a discount goldfish and in three weeks it turned green.

He bought a lifetime pen and it broke.

MY CRAZY FRIEND

He bought some handkerchiefs and they were the wrong size.

He bought some stock at 12 and it went down 15 points.

He calls for the right time and gets a wrong answer.

He calls for the weather report and the computer hangs up on him.

He got a blow-out in the spare tire in his trunk.

He got a get-sick card from his doctor.

He got some homing pigeons that don't.

He had the 24-hour virus for three weeks.

He hung up his stocking last Christmas and all he found was a note from the Health Department.

He is a poor loser, but have you ever seen a rich one?

He is a good loser; in fact, that's all he ever does.

He keeps one foot in the grave and the other on a banana peel.

He owns a ball that doesn't bounce.

He owns a banana that doesn't peel.

He owns a bell that doesn't ring.

He owns a blinker that doesn't blink.

He owns a boomerang that doesn't return.

He owns a bowling ball that doesn't roll.

He owns a broom that doesn't sweep.

He owns a bulb that doesn't light.

He owns a camera that doesn't click.

He owns a candle that doesn't burn.

He owns a car that doesn't run.

He owns a clock that doesn't work.

MY CRAZY FRIEND

He owns a door that doesn't open.

He owns a key that doesn't fit.

He owns a knife that doesn't cut.

He owns a motor that doesn't run.

He owns a parachute that doesn't open.

He owns a pen that doesn't write.

He owns a plane that doesn't fly.

He owns a radio that doesn't play.

He owns a tie that doesn't tie.

He owns a towel that doesn't dry.

He owns a violin that doesn't play.

He owns a window that doesn't close.

He owns an icebox that doesn't get cold.

He owns an umbrella that doesn't open.

He owns glue that doesn't hold.

He owns leaky galoshes.

He owns scissors that don't cut.

He owns soap that doesn't clean.

He put a seashell to his ear and got a busy signal.

He spent his lifetime paying off a cemetery plot and then drowned at sea.

His artificial flower died.

His fireproof safe burned down.

His gold watch turned green.

His goldfish got seasick.

His goldfish is allergic to water.

His heating pad never gets warm.
His hot water bottle is leaking.

MY CRAZY FRIEND

His 100-year-old turtle died.

His safe-deposit box at the bank is missing.

His self-winding watch is three days slow.

His sundial is slow.

His swimming pool burned down.

His thermos bottle is leaking.

His toupee is going bald.

His watchdog was stolen.

His waterproof basement is flooded.

He is a careful driver. Always slows down when passing a red light.

He is a cave man. Two drinks and he caves in.

He is a chain smoker. Can't afford cigarettes.

He is a fine broth of a man. Too bad some of his noodles are missing.

He is a folk singer. Always singing to his folks.

He is a gentleman farmer. Owns two station wagons and a flower pot.

He is a man of letters. Works for the post office.

He is a man of rare gifts. Hasn't given one in years.

He is a man with troubles. I think he's allergic to himself.

He is a model husband, but not a working model.

He is a pain in the neck and some people have even a lower opinion of him.

He is a person who is going places—and the sooner the better.

He is a real genius. He can do anything but make a living.

He is a real lawyer. In fact, he even named his daughter Sue.

He is a real pusher. He goes in a revolving door behind you and gets out ahead of you.

He is a steady worker. If he were any steadier he'd be motionless.

He is a student of music. Knows every bar within 10 miles of here.

He is a very friendly guy. Even shakes hands with the doorknob.

He is a very responsible person. Every time something goes wrong, he is responsible.

He is a writer worth watching—not reading, just watching!

He is always around when he needs you.

He is always kissing girls' hands. Not that he likes it, but he's crazy about hand lotion.

He is always putting his foot down—on somebody's toes.

He is always swallowing razor blades. I think he wants to sharpen his appetite.

He is an accountant, but he can't figure out his wife.

He is an artist who paints nothing but modern art. His model has the hiccups.

He is an early bird who never catches the worm.

He is at the age when he is:

Too young for a car and too old for a bike.

Too young for checks and too old for cash.

Too young for credit cards and too old for an allowance.

Too young for Excedrin and too old for children's aspirin.

Too young for his second childhood and too old for his first.

Too young for old-age pension and too old for income tax exemption.

Too young for pension and too old for passion.

Too young for Playboy Bunnies and too old for Easter Bunnies.

Too young for Serutan and too old for Castor Oil.

Too young to be left alone and too old to be left alone with a baby sitter.

Too young to be retired and too old to be fired.

Too young to drink coffee and too old to drink milk from the bottle.

Too young to get a job and too old to be a juvenile delinquent.

Too young to get married and too old to be adopted.

Too young to request a loan and too old to ask his father for money.

Too young to swear and too old to cry.

Too young to take up golf and too old to rush up to the net.

He is dark and handsome. When it's dark, he's handsome.

He is fond of high living, so he sleeps on the roof.

He is getting round shoulders from kissing short girls.

He is getting so accustomed to being tense that when he's calm he gets nervous.

He is glad they named him Bill because everybody calls him by that name.

He is having business troubles. Can't mind his own.

He is in the going-away business. You give him a dollar and he goes away.

He is just like a summer cold. You can't get rid of him.

He is knock-kneed, cross-eyed, overweight and stupid—and those are his good points.

He is known as a small-talk expert. If there's nothing to be said, he'll say it.

He is known as the VIB. Very insisting bore.

He is listed in **Who's Who** under "What's That?"

He is living proof that a man can live without a brain.

He is not a bad fellow until you get to know him.

He is not a heavy drinker. Weighs only about 130 pounds.

He is not a liar. He just arranges the truth in his favor.

He is not a very good singer, but people like to watch his Adam's apple go up and down.

He is not a very steady drinker. His hands shake too much.

He is one of those guys that when you first meet him you don't like him, but after you get to know him you hate him.

He is one of those people who pat you on your back before your face and hit you in the eye behind your back.

He is ready for television. His face is already blurred.

He is so anemic that when a mosquito lands on him, all it gets is practice.

He is so bald, his head keeps slipping off the pillow at night.

He is so bashful, he wouldn't even whistle at a taxi.

He is so boring, girls even kiss him to shut his mouth.

He is so cheap:

After shaking your hand he counts his fingers.

Before counting his money he gets drunk so he'll see double.

Before he buys drinks for the house, he makes sure he is the only one at the bar.

Even his 8 by 10 photos are only 7 by 9.

Even if he were in a canoe he wouldn't tip.

For supper he sits on the porch and bites his lips.

He always counts his money in front of a mirror so he won't cheat himself.

He always licks his eyeglasses after eating grapefruit.

He always swallows his food without chewing so he won't wear out his teeth.

He always takes long steps to save on shoe leather.

He always washes his paper plates.

He always wears mittens so money won't slip through his fingers.

He bought a watermelon, put some feathers on it and told his children it was a turkey.

He bought his daughter a doll house with a mortgage on it.

He called up his girl to find out which night she would be free.

He decided to become a divorce lawyer so he could get women free.

He even stops his watch to save time.

He fed his cat salted peanuts so it would drink water instead of milk.

He gave his children violin lessons so they wouldn't have to get haircuts.

He gave his wife a one-month subscription to **Reader's Digest**.

He goes to a drugstore and buys one Kleenex.

He got married in his own backyard so his chicken could have the rice.

He has a coin slot on his bathroom door for visitors.

He has a slight impediment in his reach.

He heats his knives so he won't use too much butter.

He is tighter than the top olive in the bottle.

He is waiting for a total eclipse of the sun so he can send a night-rate telegram.

He is waiting for the **Encyclopedia Britannica** to come out in paperback.

He keeps a moth as a pet because it only eats holes.

He keeps his fingernails extra short so he has a hard time picking up a check.

He learned Braille so he could read in the dark.

He left his home town as a barefoot boy and came back 10 years later for his shoes.

He married a girl born February 29th, so he only had to buy her a birthday present every four years.

He married a skinny girl so he could buy a small wedding ring.

He married his secretary so he wouldn't have to give her a Christmas bonus.

He never eats asparagus in a restaurant so he won't have to leave tips.

He never enjoys dessert in a restaurant. It's too close to the check.

He never wears suspenders or a belt so he has to keep his hands in his pockets.

He rides the subway during rush hours to get his clothes pressed.

He opened his wallet once and three moths flew out.

He puts green glasses on his horses to make them believe the straw he feeds them is grass.

He puts boric acid in his grapefruit to get a free eyewash.

He puts glue in his mustache so his kisses will last longer.

He quit golf when he lost his ball.

He reaches for a check like it was a subpoena.

He remarried his wife so he wouldn't have to pay any more alimony.

He re-threads his old shoelaces.

He saved all his toys for his second childhood.

He says his prayers once a year and the rest of the year he only says: "ditto."

He shakes hands with one finger.

He shot his parents so he could go to an orphan's picnic.

He shows his children a picture of a cake on their birthdays.

He spends hours in front of his TV set, but he will never turn it on.

He takes his electric razor to the office to recharge it.

He takes his girl to a drive-in restaurant and then won't open the windows.

He talks through his nose to save wear and tear on his teeth.

MY CRAZY FRIEND

He tears the month of December off his calendar to fool his children.

He thinks he's treating when he pays his own check.

He told his kids that Santa Claus doesn't make house calls anymore.

He took his children out of school because they had to pay attention.

He took his girl for a taxi ride and she was so beautiful, he could hardly keep his eyes on the meter.

He took his girl to a movie and got so excited that he almost paid for his ticket.

He took out fire insurance on his cigars.

He tried to get a postage stamp wholesale.

He uses the same calendar year after year.

He waits for an eclipse to develop his film.

He walks his date to a drive-in movie.

He holds an umbrella over his sheep when it rains so the wool won't shrink.

He only wears clothes with one-way pockets.

He went alone on his honeymoon.

He will always sit with his back to the check.

He will never finish his soup so that he won't have to tip the bowl.

He won't even give his wife an argument.

He won't even let you borrow trouble.

He won't even tip his hat.

He won't laugh unless it is at somebody else's expense.

He won't send his pajamas to the laundry unless he has a pair of socks stuck in the pocket.

MY CRAZY FRIEND

He won't take a drink out of a bottle because it has to be tipped.

He would come over and borrow a flag on July 4th.

He would give a nudist a pocket watch.

He would have asked for separate checks at the Last Supper.

He would never even pass the buck.

He would stick his head into a Mix Master to save the price of a haircut.

He wouldn't even spend Christmas.

In fact, he is tighter than a train window.

The last time he picked up a dinner check was at McDonald's.

The only thing he ever gave away was a secret.

The only thing he ever paid was a compliment.

The only thing he ever saved for a rainy day was his vacation.

The only thing he ever threw out was the bill collector.

The only thing he ever took out was his teeth.

The only things he puts on the table when company comes are ashtrays.

The only time he puts his own hands in his pockets is on cold days.

The only time he will pick up a check is when it is made out to him.

They were married 35 years and the last present he gave his wife was a wedding ring.

To save feeding them he sent his flock of homing pigeons out, and then moved.

MY CRAZY FRIEND

To save money on his laundry bill, he puts soap flakes in all his pockets and walks through a carwash once a week.

When he found a box of Contac he tried to catch a cold.

When he found a box of corn plasters he went out and bought a pair of tight shoes.

When he pays you a compliment he asks for a receipt.

When he says he's eating out he means eating on the fire escape.

When he sends Christmas cards they read: "A Merry Christmas for all coming years!"

He is so conceited, he always sings: "The best things in life are me!"

He is so disagreeable that his own shadow won't keep him company.

He is so dull, he couldn't even entertain a doubt.

He is so fancy, he eats ice cream with knife and fork.

He is so filthy rich, everybody wants to take him to the cleaners.

He is so henpecked, he cackles in his sleep.

He is so henpecked, he hasn't heard his own voice for 10 years.

He is so henpecked, he not only brings home the bacon, he cooks it.

He is so henpecked, he still takes orders from his first wife.

He is so henpecked, the only time he opens his mouth is to ask his wife where the mop is.

He is so honest, he worked in a Turkish bath for two years and never took one.

MY CRAZY FRIEND

He is so lazy:

He always goes through a revolving door on some-one else's push.

He always runs his car over a bump just to knock the ashes off his cigar.

He always wears a loafer jacket.

He asked a travel office to find him some nice scenic spot within 200 yards of his home.

He bought a book on exercise and then lay down on the couch to read it.

He claims he has a bad case of insomnia because he keeps waking every second day.

He cooks his breakfast on the electric blanket in bed.

He could fall asleep in the middle of a nap.

He couldn't catch a cold in Alaska.

He does his reading in autumn because the season turns the leaves.

He doesn't even lift his eyebrow.

He doesn't even take time out to write home for money.

He doesn't walk in his sleep. He hitchhikes.

He doesn't walk in his sleep. He insists on being carried.

He even eats loaf bread.

He even drives a shiftless car.

He even hired a man to take care of his window plants.

He even hired someone to snore for him.

He even married a widow with five children.

MY CRAZY FRIEND

He even takes a sleeping pill the first thing in the morning.

He gets into a revolving door and waits.

He goes to a picnic and takes along pre-toasted marshmallows.

He had the seven-year itch and was six years behind in scratching.

He is getting up every day at 5 a.m. to have more time to loaf.

He is whittling with an electric knife.

He joined five unions, so he's always on strike.

He never puts anything off until tomorrow. He puts it off forever.

He only does what he does best—sleep.

He only opens his mouth to put something in it.

He only throws kisses.

He only washes his ears when he eats watermelons.

He puts a tea bag in his mustache and drinks hot water.

He puts popcorn in his pancakes so they'll turn over by themselves.

He reaches for the stool when a piano has to be moved.

He runs for the bus and his feet fall asleep.

He was born with a silver spoon in his mouth and hasn't stirred since.

He will hold a cocktail shaker and wait days for an earthquake.

He won't even exercise discretion.

He won't even hang up the telephone.

He wouldn't even help his mother-in-law move out of the house.

He wouldn't even shake the limb if money grew on trees.

He wouldn't even steal a kiss from a beautiful girl.

He is so mean:

He only walks old women halfway across the street.

He would steal the last fan from a fan dancer.

He is so nervous, he can thread a needle in a sewing machine while it is running.

He is so old:

Even his tongue turned gray.

He gets winded turning on his TV set.

He has to bend down twice to pick up something once.

He still chases women, but can't remember why.

When he walks he creaks and when he talks he squeaks.

You have to remind him to renew his subscription to **Playboy**.

He is so polite, he will always take his hat off when he mentions his own name.

He is so polite, he will always take his shoes off before putting his feet on the coffee table.

He is so polite, he wouldn't open an oyster without knocking on the shell first.

He is so small, they offered him a job in a piggy bank.

He is so strong, he bends spoons stirring the coffee.

He is so strong, he can tear a phone book in half the hard way—one page at a time.

He is so superstitious, he has the feeling he was born under a ladder.

He is so tall, he has to stand on a chair to brush his teeth.

He is so tough:

He eats sardines without removing the can.

He uses a barbed wire as a hairnet.

He uses barbed wire as dental floss.

He washes his face with steel wool.

He is so unlucky, he runs into accidents which started out happening to someone else.

He is so unlucky, if it rained soup he'd have a fork in his hand.

He is so weak:

He has to starch his legs so they won't wobble.

He has to use both hands to brush his teeth.

He needs help to open the refrigerator.

He needs help to tie his shoelaces.

He needs help to turn on the TV set.

He is such a bad piano player, whenever he plays the national anthem people sit down.

He is such a bore that people have parties just not to have him.

He is such a poor artist, he can't even draw a curtain.

He is such a poor artist, the only thing he can draw properly is his bath.

He is such a quiet dresser, he won't even allow tongues in his shoes.

He is such an egoist, he joined the navy so the world could see him.

He is such an insomniac that when he's sleeping he dreams he's not sleeping.

He is very clever. Always puts his problems away for a brainy day.

He is the kind of man who picks his friends to pieces.

He is the kind of man who will borrow your pot to cook your goose.

He is the kind of man who will stand on a bread line and ask for toast.

He is the kind of man who would eat a frankfurter on a hamburger roll.

He is the kind of man who would hide your teeth and then offer you corn on the cob.

He is the kind of man who would steal a dead fly from a blind spider.

He is the kind of man you'd use as a blueprint to build an idiot.

He is the master of the house and has his wife's permission to say so.

He is the only fellow who looks as bad as his passport photo.

He is the only fellow who speaks Scotch with a soda accent.

He is the only man who wears sunglasses to protect his eyes from the glare of his nose.

He is too short for work as a longshoreman and too tall to be a short-order cook.

He is very intellectual. He can bore you on any subject.

He is very musical. As a child he played on the floor. Now he plays on the piano.

He is very particular about what he drinks. It has to be liquid.

He is very sensitive about his hair. I don't know why—he hasn't got any.

He is vulgar, arrogant and has bad breath—and those are his good points!

He is what you may call a light drinker. He drinks until it gets light.

He just found happiness in the dictionary. It's under booze.

He just installed a new loudspeaker in his house. He got married again.

He keeps 200 clocks around the house since he heard that time is valuable.

He kept chewing gum on the train because the engine said: "Choo-choo!"

He kisses his wife only when he can't find a napkin.

He kissed so many girls he can do it with his eyes closed.

He knows a great deal about nothing and nothing about a great deal.

He learned the "Wedding March" backwards and now sings it at divorces.

He likes to tinker around the house. In fact, he's the biggest tinker in town.

He looks as comfortable as a centipede with athlete's foot.

He lost control of his car. He couldn't keep up the payments.

He lost over 100 pounds in one week. His wife left him.

He loved her so much he worshipped the ground her father struck oil on.

He made his dog sit in the sun to get a hot dog.

He always makes money at the racetrack. He sells cold drinks.

He manufactured slipcovers for pianos.

He manufactures ashes. Just give him a cigar and watch.

He married a girl who had everything—even twins.

He married my sister. Now he hates me like a brother.

He met a girl in a revolving door and has been going around with her ever since.

He moved to the city when he heard the country was at war.

He must use an electric razor. He has a face only a motor could love.

He never drinks coffee in the morning. It keeps him awake all day.

He only drinks for one reason. It's cheaper than sending his wife to the beauty parlor.

He only gets homesick when he is home.

He only knows two tunes. One is "Yankee Doodle" and the other isn't.

He only opens his mouth when he has nothing to say.

He only plays golf to aggravate himself.

He promised his wife to bring home the bacon but it was a lot of bologna.

He put an electric toaster in his mattress so he could pop out of bed easily.

He put his radio into the refrigerator to get cool music.

He put his wine on top of the house to keep up his spirits.

He put some iodine in his wallet because he got a cut in his salary.

He put some vitamins in his gin. He claims they build him up while he is tearing himself down.

He puts on a blindfold when he goes on a blind date.

He put on a wet shirt because the label said: "Wash and wear."

He refused to sleep with his wife because she was a married woman.

He reminds me of London—always in a fog.

He runs a broken down fix-it shop.

He runs everything but the vacuum cleaner.

He saved all the money he would have spent on beer and finally spent it on beer.

He sleeps only four hours. Yes, only four hours, but three times a day.

He slept the whole week in the sewer. It was the only place he could get a room with running water.

He solved his parking problem. He swapped his car for 300 subway tokens.

He speaks straight from the shoulder. He has a very short neck.

He spends his spare time doing useful things—like walking down an UP escalator.

He spilled some beer on the stove. Now he has foam on the range.

He started working for peanuts until he proved his salt. Now he works for salted peanuts.

He suffers from an occupational disease. Work makes him sick.

He thinks he's a big cheese, but he only smells like that.

He took his girl for a ride and had motor trouble. His car wouldn't stall.

He took his girl to a barn dance and she gave him the old stall.

He took his misfortune like a man. He blamed it on his wife.

He took the bus home after work, but his wife made him take it back.

He tried to be a gentleman farmer, but he failed in both capacities.

He tried to learn how to ski, but by the time he learned how to stand, he couldn't sit down.

He wanted a big house with a big car and wound up with a big wife with a big mouth.

He wanted to start a third party because he was thrown out of two.

He was a boy scout until he was fifteen, then he became a girl scout.

He was a colorful fighter—black and blue all over.

He was a daydreaming night watchman.

He was afraid to talk turkey because he was chicken.

He was born modest, but it didn't last.

He was born on April 2—just one day too late.

He was born stupid and lately he had a relapse.

He was born upside down. His nose runs and his feet smell.

He was condemned to be hanged, but he saved his life by dying in prison.

He was elected chairman of the meeting. He had to set up the chairs.

He was probably the best boxer in the country, but he always got beaten in the city.

He was so absentminded:

He changed his oil every day and his shirt every 2,000 miles.

He complained to his wife that his secretary didn't understand him.

He courted a girl and charged her two dollars a visit.

He cut his finger and forgot to bleed.

He danced with the mop and mopped the floor with his wife.

He dictated to a cigar and got his secretary lit.

He dictated to his dog and tried to give his stenographer a bath.

He even held the door open for his own wife when nobody was looking.

He fell overboard and forgot to swim.

He gave his bride two dollars and kissed the minister at the wedding.

He got on his bike backwards and complained that someone stole the handlebars.

He got up and struck a match to see if he had blown out the candle.

He held an egg in his hand and boiled his watch.

He hid his face in his hands and forgot where to look for it.

He hitched his wife to the plow and kissed the horse goodbye.

He kissed a football and threw a baby.

He kissed his dishes good night and threw his wife into the sink.

He kissed his model and chiseled on his wife.

He kissed his own wife under the mistletoe.

He kissed his pants goodbye and took his wife to the cleaners.

He kissed the door goodbye and slammed his wife going out.

He locked his wife in the garage and kissed his car good night.

He opened his bed and jumped out the window.

He parked his car in front of the finance company.

He picked up a snake and hit the stick.

He poured syrup down his back and scratched his pancakes.

He powdered his shoe and shined his nose.

He put his dog to bed and let himself out the backdoor.

He put his pants to bed and hung over the chair all night.

He put his umbrella to bed and stood in the sink all night.

He put salt on his dog and patted the mashed potatoes.

He put the candle to bed and blew himself out.

He rolled under the dresser and waited for his collar button to find him.

He said "goodbye" to the plane and ran after his girl.

He said "good morning" to the time clock and punched his boss.

He scratched his wife and kissed the match.

He sent his dog to camp and his child to obedience school.

He sent his mail to the golf course and played all day with his secretary.

He sent his wife to the bank and kissed his money goodbye.

He spent an hour looking for his cuff links, then he remembered he was wearing a short-sleeved shirt.

He stood in front of a mirror trying to remember where he'd seen himself before.

He stopped his girl and went too far with his car.

He talked to a grapefruit and squeezed the maid.

He threw his clothes on the bed and lay down in the closet.

He threw his pants in the bathtub and hanged himself in the closet.

He took a course to improve his memory and forgot where the school was.

He took his car for a walk and left his girl to be washed and polished.

He took his wife to a nightclub and phoned his secretary to tell her he had to work late.

He took his wife to dinner instead of his secretary.

He tucked his waffle under his chin and ate the napkin.

He poured catsup on his shoelaces and tied bows in his spaghetti.

He was so busy earning his salt he forgot his sugar.

He wears a wrist compass so he can tell whether he's coming or going.

He went up to a horse at the races and bet two dollars on a bookie.

He wound up the cat, put out his wife and got into bed with the clock.

He was so dumb:

He always asked what wine went best with Alpo.

He always got lost going up on an escalator.

He bought a blank bumper sticker. He didn't want to get involved.

He could write the story of his life on a piece of confetti.

He couldn't solve a jigsaw puzzle if it only had two pieces.

He had a brain concussion and it was classified as a minor injury.

He handed a drowning man a glass of water.

He invited a mermaid to a fish fry.

He lit a match to read his sundial.

He liked his fried chicken broiled.

He ordered chicken at Napoleon's restaurant so he could pull the bone apart.

He saved burnt-out light bulbs for his darkroom.

He slept on his water bed wearing a life jacket.

He slept with his alarm clock under his pillow so he could get up on time.

He swallowed a firecracker so his hair would grow out in bangs.

He swallowed pennies so there would be some change in him.

He took a taxi every day just to tell someone where to go.

He thought a cotton gin was a furry martini.

He thought he was hard-boiled when he was only half-baked.

He thought a chocolate bar was a bar where they served hot chocolate.

He thought a fire commissioner got a commission on every fire.

He thought a fire engine was an engine that created fires.

He thought a firehouse was a place where they kept fire.

He thought a fireplace was a place where you got fired.

He thought a fire sale was a place to buy some fires.

He threw away his socks because they weren't worth a darn.

He tiptoed into the drugstore so he wouldn't wake the sleeping pills.

He took a bicycle to bed so he wouldn't have to walk in his sleep.

He took a hammer to bed so he could hit the hay.

He took a ladder to the party because he heard the drinks were on the house.

He took a nap in the chandelier because he was a light sleeper.

He took a ruler to bed to see how long he slept.

He tried to rob tourists coming back from Las Vegas.

He tried to write a chain letter but his pen kept slipping off the chain.

He used two hands to brush his teeth. He held the toothbrush in one hand and pushed his head back and forth with the other.

MY CRAZY FRIEND

He wanted to be open-minded, so he blew his brain out.

He wanted to buy a two-piece jigsaw puzzle.

He wanted to buy an air-conditioner for his motorcycle.

He wanted to die with his boots on so he wouldn't hurt his toes when he kicked the bucket.

He wanted to get a charge out of life, so he studied electricity.

He wanted to go jogging in Venice.

He wanted to be cremated because he didn't believe in death.

He wanted to work in a bank. He thought there was money in it.

He was in the restaurant business, but he had to give it up. All the dishes got dirty.

He was running around the bed trying to catch some sleep.

He was so proud of a gold medal, he had it bronzed.

He was staying up all night trying to figure out where the sun went when it went down. Finally it dawned on him.

He was trying to sell Venetian blinds to submarines.

He went blind drinking coffee. He always left the spoon in the cup.

He went to a camera store to rent some flashbulbs.

He went to a doctor to get a hernia transplant.

He went to a nudist camp blindfolded.

He went to the country to see a barn dance.

When he found some nail polish he went out and bought some nails.

When the doctor told him to strip to the waist he dropped his pants.

He was so nearsighted he couldn't tell the North Pole from the South Pole.

He was so poor:

He bought a piggy bank and then had no money left to put in it.

He bought only one shoe at a time.

He bought postage stamps on the installment plan.

He could afford only one lifeguard for his swimming pool.

He could have only one measle at a time.

He couldn't afford an overcoat so he had to go to Florida for the winter.

He couldn't afford to go window shopping.

He couldn't afford to hire a special cook for his chauffeurs.

He didn't even have his own ZIP code.

He didn't have a house, just a door.

He had a wind-up TV set.

He had his hearing aid on a party line.

He had only one pay phone in his Cadillac.

He had to build his penthouse in the basement.

He had to raise his own caviar.

He had to postpone a few meals.

He had to wash his Cadillac himself.

He had to watch TV by candlelight.

He had wall-to-wall nothing.

He stuffed his turkey with newspapers.

He thought a knife and fork were jewelry.

He used old newspaper as wall-to-wall carpeting.

He walked to the opera twice a week to save carfare.

He was 14 when he found out that people eat three meals a day.

His wife had to wear last year's jewelry.

He was so rich:

At parties he only served money.

For his honeymoon he took a trip around his safe.

He always showed movies in his Cadillac.

He bathed in his solid gold bathtub and left a 14-karat ring.

He bought his son an air-conditioned baby carriage.

He bought his son a bicycle with whitewall tires.

He bought his son a chemistry outfit—DuPont.

He bought his son a doctor-nurse outfit—a hospital.

He bought his son a fishing outfit—a rod, a reel and a river.

He bought his son a kiddie car with built-in telephone.

He bought his son a pipe—a pipe that carries oil from Alaska to Texas.

He bought his son a set of trains—the Pennsylvania and the Central.

He built a house with seven dining rooms—one for each course.

He bought a new typewriter whenever he needed a new ribbon.

MY CRAZY FRIEND

He changed shoelaces every day.

He carried an attaché case filled with credit cards.

He could drive 20 miles and never leave his garage.

He could retire and live off the interests of his interests.

He didn't count his money. He weighed it.

He didn't need air-conditioned Cadillacs. He kept them in a freezer.

He didn't paint Easter eggs. He wallpapered them.

He even got a boy for his dog.

He even went to a drive-in movie in a taxi.

He got a green thumb from counting money.

He had a bank named after him.

He had a bathroom with a picture window.

He had a bathtub with a golden ring.

He had a bicycle made by Cadillac.

He had a bookkeeper who only counted his money.

He had a butler who had his own butler.

He had a car with an unlisted number.

He had a car with a built-in barbecue pit.

He had a chauffeur-driven sled.

He had a dentist for each tooth.

He had a few money belts on the clothesline.

He had a fur-lined bathing suit.

He had a glass-covered golf course.

He had a golden Yo-Yo.

He had a house so big, when it was 8 o'clock in the kitchen, it was 10 o'clock in the bathroom.

He had a kidney-shaped swimming pool, a heart-shaped patio, and a funny-shaped garage.

He had a kitchen with five rooms.

He had a little piggy bank—The First National.

He had a sleep-in banker.

He had a special safe just for his credit cards.

He had a special suit just for the moths.

He had a special upholsterer to stuff his turkey.

He had a split-level Cadillac.

He had a station wagon that was bigger than the station.

He had a terrible nightmare. He dreamed he only had one million.

He had a walk-in mailbox.

He had a walk-in wallet.

He had a wallpapered refrigerator.

He had an air-conditioned steam room.

He had an air-conditioned swimming pool.

He had an 18-hole golf course in his recreation room.

He had an elevator with a built-in bar.

He had an office on an unlisted floor.

He had an unlisted mailbox.

He had an unlisted number in Sing Sing.

He had an unlisted Social Security number.

He had an unlisted wife.

He had an unlisted ZIP code number.

He had all Cadillacs marked His or Hers.

He had all his money tied up in cash.

MY CRAZY FRIEND

He had ashtrays on his motorcycle.

He had bookcases filled with bankbooks.

He had contact lenses with golden frames.

He had four bartenders behind his basement bar.

He had four cars—one for each direction.

He had four cars—one for each season.

He had his car wallpapered inside and outside.

He had his garage papered with 1000-dollar bills.

He had his own sleep-in TV repairman.

He had Kleenex made-to-order.

He had mink lining in his sable coat.

He had monogrammed money.

He had monogrammed toothpicks.

He had more money than his wife could spend.

He had phones in every closet.

He had rings under his eyes with diamonds in them.

He had separate calendars for each day of the week.

He had solid gold silverware.

He had stained-glass contact lenses.

He had suits that cost $100 just to clean.

He had Swiss money in an American bank.

He had three swimming pools: one with salt water, one with sweet water and one with seltzer.

He had to buy a new rug. Somebody stepped on the old one.

He had to buy another yacht. The first one got wet.

He had to give away his new Cadillac. The ashtrays were full.

He had to pay storage charges for his bankbooks.

He had to wear suspenders to keep up his money belt.

He had two arm chairs—one for each arm.

He had two brokers—Stock and Pawn.

He had two cars—one for driving and one for parking.

He had two chauffeurs—one only made left turns.

He had two desks—one for each foot.

He had two hot-water bottles—one for each foot.

He had two nose specialists—one for each nostril.

He had two secretaries—one for each knee.

He had two swimming pools—one just for rinsing.

He had two toothbrushes—one for the upper and one for the lower.

He had used $100 bills just to soundproof his music room.

He had wall-to-wall bankbooks.

He had wall-to-wall carpeting in his swimming pool.

He had wall-to-wall carpeting in his garage.

He had wall-to-wall furniture.

He had wall-to-wall parties.

He had wall-to-wall money.

He had a three-room safe deposit box.

He had music in all his elevators—live bands.

He had to pay overweight for his moneybelt whenever he traveled by plane.

He hired a chauffeur for his lawn mower.

MY CRAZY FRIEND

He hired a chauffeur for his motorcycle.

He hired someone to sleep for him.

He hired a man to play golf with him.

He was always ahead in his alimony payments.

He kept a Volkswagen in the trunk of his Cadillac.

He never found out whose picture is on the one-dollar bill.

He never walked in his sleep. He took a taxi.

He played ball in his ballroom.

He put a fire hydrant in his living room to keep his dogs off the street.

He spent his summers in a little place he bought up north—Canada.

He used a motorboat to cross his swimming pool.

He was worried about his little son. The baby was lost in the nursery and wasn't found for two days.

He wouldn't even ride in the same car with his chauffeur.

His bankroll was so big, he had to put it on microfilm to fit in his wallet.

His bathtub had three faucets: hot, cold and luke.

His birthday party lasted from birthday to birthday.

His Cadillacs have stained-glass windows.

His car was so big he kept a spare tire in the glove compartment.

His car was so big, it had six doors on each side.

His car was so long it took five minutes to go through a one-minute car wash.

His cars had curtains and drapes.

His charcoal grill had whitewall tires.

MY CRAZY FRIEND

His chauffeur had his own chauffeur.

His child liked to play with blocks. So he bought him Rockefeller Center.

His garbage was gift-wrapped.

His garage had wall-to-wall cars.

His house had four ZIP code numbers.

His house was so big, he used a golf cart to go from room to room.

His house was so big, the closets had picture windows.

His lawn mower had whitewall tires.

His kid's piggy bank had a vice-president.

The finance company owed him money.

The local bank opened a branch in his living room.

The snow-chains for his cars were gold-filled.

The water in his swimming pool had a permanent wave.

When he needed some oil for his hair he bought Oklahoma.

When he went to Heaven he got an unlisted harp.

When his wife got sick he bought her a Cadillac as a get-well card.

When his wife wanted a diamond, he bought her Yankee Stadium.

Whenever he bought Cadillacs he took the change in Volkswagens.

Whenever he cashed a check the bank bounced.

Whenever he ate alphabet soup he ate only his initials.

Whenever he went to a party he took along his own swimming pool.

Whenever his diamonds got dirty he bought new ones.

He was such a hypochondriac, he had three medicine chests.

He was such a hypochondriac that they buried him next to a doctor.

He was thrown out of a nudist camp because he had a coat on his tongue.

He was trying to lose annoying weight, but his wife didn't want a divorce.

He was trying to write a drinking song, but he couldn't get past the first few bars.

He watered his garden with whiskey. He wanted some stewed tomatoes.

He went on a blind date and she was just what the doctor ordered—a pill.

He went on a 14-day diet but the only thing he lost was his hair.

He went to jail for something he didn't do. He didn't pay his taxes.

He will never be too old to learn new ways to be stupid.

He will never do anything behind his wife's back except zip her up.

He worked:

as a blacksmith in a candy store. He had to shoo flies.

as a boxer at the railroad. He had to punch tickets.

as a brush salesman so he could lead a fuller life.

as a candlemaker—only on wick ends.

as a cashier in a piggy bank.

as a census taker. He went from house to house increasing the population.

as a cruise director on a ferry.

as a deckhand on a submarine.

as a decorator in a paper factory. He made curtains for window envelopes.

as a dentist in a bakery. He put fillings in chocolate eclairs.

as a director in a bank. Had to direct people to the safes.

as a draft clerk in a bank. Had to open and close windows.

as a farmhand in a candy factory. Had to milk chocolates.

as a fortuneteller, but he saw no future in it.

as a garbage collector, until his cold cleared up.

as a garbage truck driver. Thirty dollars a week and all he could eat.

as a gardener in a cocktail lounge. He had to water the liquor.

as a gardener on a dairy farm. He watered milk.

as a grease monkey, but there's no future in greasing monkeys.

as a haberdasher for the railroad. He was in charge of the ties.

as a headwaiter on a tugboat.

as a holdup man. He sold suspenders.

as a jeweler at the ballpark. He had to clean the diamond.

as a keyman. If you wanted to go to the washroom he handed you the key.

as a kite salesman. All day he told people to go and fly a kite.

as a lifeguard at a water mattress factory.

as a lifeguard in a motor pool.

as a meatpacker. He sold girdles.

as a mechanic at a racetrack. He fixed races.

as a mechanic in a candy factory. He had to tighten the nuts in the chocolate bars.

as a mechanic in a sardine factory. Every 1000 miles he changed the oil.

as a newspaper reporter. He had to report how many papers were left on the stands.

as a night watchman in a day camp.

as a night watchman. Then someone stole two nights and he was fired.

as a novelty worker. It was a novelty when he worked.

as a panhandler. He was an intern in a hospital.

as a piano mover, but he couldn't even carry a tune.

as a plumber in a tobacco shop. He took care of the pipes.

as a police reporter. Every week he had to report to the police.

as a prize fighter in a candy store. He had to box chocolates.

as a professional reader. He read gas meters.

as a quick-change artist in a penny arcade.

as a smoker in a fish market. He smoked herrings.

as a snuff salesman. He went around putting his business in other people's noses.

as a social director on a freight train.

as a street cleaner, but he couldn't keep his mind in the gutter.

as a swimming instructor in a car pool.

as a tailor in a lawyer's office. He pressed suits.

as a taxidermist in a voting place. He had to stuff ballots.

as a telephone operator in a laundry. Had to wring towels.

as a teller in a blood bank.

as a traffic director in a phone booth.

as a waiter in a courthouse. He had to serve summonses.

as a window washer in a submarine.

as a window washer. Too bad he had to step back to admire his work.

as a worm imitator. He had to bore holes in antique furniture.

as an electrician in a bakery. He had to put currants in the cinnamon buns.

as an elevator man—sort of human Yo-Yo.

as an elevator operator, but he couldn't remember the route.

as an independent salesman. He took orders from no one.

as an oculist in a restaurant kitchen. He took care of the eyes of potatoes.

as an operator of a candy store. He called people to the phone.

as an umpire in a restaurant. He had to dust off plates.

at a hot dog counter. All day he had to count hot dogs.

for a doctor. He had to stand outside and make people sick.

for a government collecting agency. He drove a garbage truck.

for a sculptor. He was a very good chiseler.

for a tea company—until he asked them for a coffee break.

for a water company. Two-fifty an hour and all he could drink.

for a window-shade company. He pulled down 4000 a year.

for Breakdown Construction Company—until they broke down.

in a coffee mill, but couldn't stand the grind.

in a department store. They put him in ladies underwear.

in a distillery. For overtime he got time and a fifth.

in a grocery store. He laid eggs in the window.

in a pigeon-raising business, but it all flew out the window.

in a roadmap business, but it folded.

in a submarine factory, but it went under.

in a tie department. He had to tie up this and tie up that.

He would be in better health if he wouldn't get sick so often.

He would like to sing the song "The Clock," but he doesn't want to alarm anybody.

He writes books nobody will read and checks nobody will cash.

He wrote his girl every day so she married the mailman.

His brother broke one of the strings on his guitar and won't tell him which.

His business is now on solid foundation—on the rocks.

His car has three speeds: Slow, Fast and Yes Your Honor.

His car is in first-crash condition.

His car is so old it needs upper and lower plates.

His car is so old the insurance covers fire, theft and Indian raids.

His car was so old that every time he went to the finance company to make a payment he had to go by taxi.

His credit rating is so bad his cash isn't even accepted.

His doctor told him to give up golf and his golf instructor told him the same thing.

His eyes were never good and he has a wife to prove it.

His face is his fortune. That's why he pays no income tax.

His father was an electrician and he was his first shock.

His friends call it 'Madness.' But he calls it golf!

His hobby is collecting old echoes.

His idea of a fine vacation is to rest in the shade of a beautiful blonde.

His idea of a seven-course dinner is a hamburger and a six-pack.

His idea of an exciting night is to turn up his electric blanket.

His I.Q. finally caught up with his eyesight—20:20.

His jokes are not funny, but his delivery is terrible.

His life is so dull he looks forward to a dental appointment.

His mind is in great shape. He rarely uses it.

His mind is so small, it would ruin your eyes trying to read it.

His mind may be slow, but it's dull.

His monthly salary runs into three figures: his wife and two children.

His mother should have thrown him away and kept the stork.

His nose is so big, while walking in France he got a cold in England.

His nose is so lazy it won't even run when he has a cold.

His speech started at 8 sharp and ended at 10 flat.

His trousers are shabby and worn but they cover a warm heart.

His weekly earnings run into four figures: $89.95.

His wit is about as sharp as a dull toothache.

2

My
Silly
Girl

Her car won't start running and her nose won't stop.

Her charge plates and credit cards are killing me.

Her children are doing so badly in school, she goes to
PTA meetings under an assumed name.

Her dress looked pretty good considering the shape it
was on.

Her eyes can flash like a railroad crossing signal.

Her face can turn milk sour.

Her face, figure and voice make you stop, look and
listen.

Her face is calm as custard.

Her face is her fortune and it runs into a nice figure.

Her face may be her fortune, but the other parts draw
interest.

Her family is so exclusive. They didn't come over on the Mayflower, they had their own boat.

Her figure? She looks more like a bottle of milk than a bottle of Coke.

Her gossip is so interesting you always wish you could know the person she is talking about.

Her gown reminds me of a fine song—sweet and low!

Her gown reminds me of Texas. Plenty of wide open spaces.

Her hair color changed so often she has a convertible top.

Her heart belongs to me, but the rest of her goes out with other guys.

Her mouth is so big:

Every time she opens it her tongue falls out.

Her dentist can work with both hands in her mouth.

It has an echo.

It's bigger than her appetite.

It takes her an hour to put on lipstick.

It takes two men to kiss her.

She can eat a banana sideways.

She can eat three meatballs at once.

She can finish a watermelon in three bites.

She can kiss your mouth and your forehead at the same time.

She can play a trumpet from either side.

She can sing duets by herself.

She can whisper in her own ear.

She drank Coca-Cola and swallowed the bottle.

She eats a minute steak in 20 seconds.

She gets her toothbrush made to order.

She has room for 20 more teeth.

She has to put on her lipstick with a roller.

She keeps her toothbrush in a violin case.

She kissed a fellow and bit off his nose.

She kisses with only one lip.

She needs a full hour to brush her teeth.

She needs a size 20 lipstick.

She needs both hands to cover her mouth when she yawns.

She rents it out as a fly catcher.

She smiled and got lipstick on her ears.

She yawned and her ears disappeared.

The doctor had to use an ironing board as tongue depressor.

When she wants a small picture she has to keep her mouth closed.

Her mouth is so small, she uses a shoehorn to take an aspirin.

Her parents are in the iron and steel business. Her mother irons and her father steals.

Her perfume is nothing to sniff at.

Her voice sounds like a garbage disposal with a spoon caught in it.

She's a nurse? She couldn't even put dressing on a salad.

She admitted she was 40, but she didn't say when.

She always cleans the mirror. Who wants to see dirty wrinkles?

She always drives very slowly. She will do anything to stay under 30.

She always flirts with the butcher—playing for bigger steaks.

She always looks like she dressed in front of an airplane propeller.

She always smiles. No wonder she has sunburned teeth.

She always speaks twice before she thinks.

She always wears a dress with a square neck—to go with her head.

She always wears a red dress to match her nose.

She always wears silk dresses because she doesn't want the wool pulled over her eyes.

She ate her birthday cake so fast, the lit candles burned her mouth.

She belongs in the top 500. She is one of the zeros.

She bought a book on reducing and all she lost was the price of the book.

She bought a Ship-and-Shore blouse and then discovered she didn't have the coastline for it.

She calls her dress 'Opportunity' because there's plenty of room on the top.

She calls her dress 'Thanksgiving' because it shows more meat than dressing.

She calls her off-shoulder dress 'London Bridge' because it's always falling down.

She calls her strapless gown 'Armored Car' because it's hard to hold up.

She calls it her purse, but I call it a portable attic.

She can't be two-faced or she wouldn't be wearing that one.

She can't type too well, but she can erase 50 words a minute.

She certainly has what it takes, but she has had it so long nobody wants it.

She claims she just turned 30. It must have been a U-turn.

She claims she just turned 25. Before she turned it, it was 52.

She claims she made the dress out of odds and ends. Well, it's certainly odd where it ends.

She comes from such an old family, it's been condemned.

She couldn't swim a stroke, but she knew every dive in town.

She didn't start admitting her age until she was too old to deny it.

She diets religiously—one day a week.

She doesn't care how empty her head is, as long as her sweater fits tightly.

She doesn't like prunes because it is impolite to eat and run.

She doesn't look 38—anymore.

She doesn't show her age, but if you look under her make-up, there it is!

She doesn't want to take weight off, she just wants to re-arrange it.

She dresses to be seen in the right places.

She dyed her hair so many times she has technicolor dandruff.

She eats so much her teeth get tired.

She fasted for two weeks and all she lost were two pimples.

She found the secret of youth. She lies about her age.

She once gave me a kiss that would cost $3 in a taxi.

She gave me such a hot kiss, she melted the gold in my tooth.

She gives kisses that toast your tonsils.

She goes through life standing at the complaint counter.

She had an hourglass figure and not a minute of it was wasted.

She had an impediment in her speech. It was always much too long.

She had baseball eyes—two baggers.

She had enough wrinkles on her face to hold a two-day rain.

She had hash-brown hair, blue eyes, a red face and a green thumb.

She had her face lifted, but it fell again when she saw the bill.

She had her face lifted so it would be level with her nose.

She had her face lifted so many times she talks through her nose.

She had her hair tinted red, but now it clashes with her face.

She had more ups and downs than a theater-goer in an aisle seat.

She had so much powder on her face she looked like she was in a fog.

She had such buck teeth that every time we kissed she combed my mustache.

She has a baby face and brain to match.

She has a bathing suit that fits her like a sunburn.

She has a beautiful hairdo. It looks like a floor mop in high wind.

She has a beautiful mouth. Only I wish she wouldn't keep it open so much.

She has a big appetite and a mouth to match.

She has a big heart and a stomach to match.

She has a big mouth and a head to match.

She has a big nose and ears to match.

She has a complexion like a peach—yellow and fuzzy.

She has a face like a flower—cauliflower!

She has a face like a phonograph—round, flat and full of lines.

She has a face like a pie—with cream on top.

She has a face like a poem. I don't know which line I like best.

She has a shape the world should be in.

She has calves only a cow could love.

She has everything a singer should have and a nice voice too.

She has everything. Too bad it's all in one place.

She has freckles on her tongue from eating Swiss cheese in the sun.

She has lots of polish, but only on her nails.

She has more curves than a super highway and the detours aren't bad either.

She has a face like a professional lemon taster.

She has a face like a sardine.

She has a face like a smoked herring.

She has a face like a squeezed orange.

She has a face like a street before they pour the concrete.

She has a face like a tight shoe.

She has a face like a used car. The paint conceals the age but the lines reveal the years.

She has a face like a wet holiday.

She has a face like a wet teabag.

She has a face like an unmade bed.

She has a face that could stop a sundial.

She has a face that looks like it wore out six bodies.

She has a face with everything—including a few things I never saw on a face before.

She has a face with more wrinkles than an accordion.

She has a face you don't want to remember but can't forget.

She has a figure like a bass fiddle.

She has a figure like a hippopotamus.

She has a figure like a pillow.

She has a figure that's harder to ignore than a ringing telephone.

She has a fine nose, as noses run.

She has a fine voice. I just hope someday it will reach her throat.

She has a fine voice. It ought to be fine. Every time she sings, she strains it.

She has a great sense of balance—except in her checkbook.

She has a green thumb and a face to match.

She has a heart of gold—yellow and hard.

She has a keen sense of rumor.

She has a long-playing tongue.

She has a lovely complexion. It brings out her ugliness.

MY SILLY GIRL

She has a magnetic personality. Everything is charged.

She has a memory like an elephant and a shape to match.

She has a mini-mouth and a maxi-tongue.

She has a mini-skirt, a mini-car and a mini-poodle. Why not a mini-mouth?

She has a mouth like a mailbox—open day and night.

She has a musical face—sharp in some places and flat in others.

She has a narrow mind and a waist to match.

She has a neck like a camel. It goes seven days without water.

She has a neck like a swan. Too bad it isn't as white.

She has a perfect birth control device—her face!

She has a perfect face for radio.

She has a photographic mind. Too bad it never developed.

She has a pony tail and a face to match.

She has a profile like a Greyhound bus.

She has a profile like a set of keys and a nose like a bicycle seat.

She has a Roman nose. It roams all over her face.

She has a shape like a balloon.

She has a shape like a beer barrel.

She has a shape like a piano.

She has a shape like the coastline of New Jersey, but she's too plump around Bayonne.

She has a soft heart and a head to match.

She has a Supreme Court figure—no appeal!

MY SILLY GIRL

She has a tongue like a poison arrow.

She has a tongue like a reckless driver—always running people down.

She has a tongue long enough to seal a letter after it was dropped into the mailbox.

She has a tongue long enough to wash her ears.

She has a tongue that could clip a hedge.

She has a tongue that flaps like a window shade in a summer breeze.

She has a tongue that jaywalks over every conversation.

She has a tongue that never takes a holiday. Works day after day.

She has a tongue that runs only when her brain is in neutral.

She has a truly vegetarian figure—no meat.

She has a very early American face. She looks like George Washington.

She has a very good background, and she's always leaning on it.

She has a vocabulary of only a hundred words, but she uses them over and over.

She has a voice like a broken phonograph.

She has a voice like an ambulance siren.

She has a winning smile, but a losing face.

She has a wrinkled dress and a face to match.

She has all the curves a girl could want, only on her they look like corners.

She has an empty stomach and a head to match.

She has an hourglass figure,

    but all the sand is at 8 o'clock.

but her a.m. is tremendous and her p.m. is a little behind.

but it's later than she thinks.

but she doesn't like my hands at 8:30.

but she makes every minute count.

but the sand is in the wrong places.

but the sand shifted a long time ago.

but time is running out.

She has as much personality as a pound of wet liver.

She has as much personality as a smoked herring.

She has an unusual figure. She has straight seams, but her legs are crooked.

She has antique jewelry. She got it when it was new.

She has as many curves as a scenic railway.

She has beauty in her face, if you like to read between the lines.

She has been in hot water so long, she looks like a tea bag.

She has been in more hot water than a boiled egg.

She has been on a diet for three weeks and all she's taken off is her hat.

She has been on more laps than a napkin.

She has been stood up more often than a bowling pin.

She has black hair and nails to match.

She has blue eyes and a nose to match.

She has cheeks like roses and a nose to match.

She has curves in places where other girls don't even have places.

She has early American features. She looks like a buffalo.

MY SILLY GIRL

She has ears like a shovel—always picking up dirt.

She has everything a man wants: a mustache, muscles, a beard ...

She has eyes like a limpid pool and a nose like a diving board.

She has flat feet and a head to match.

She has hazel eyes, chestnut hair, and walnut skin—what a nut!

She has long legs and a short temper.

She has lots of bounce, but you have to walk behind her to see it.

She has more wrinkles than a roadmap.

She has muscles like a truck driver.

She has musical feet—two flats.

She has everything and I wish I could get some of it back.

She has only two faults—everything she says and everything she does.

She has shiny shoes and a nose to match.

She has skin like marble and a head to match.

She has so many cavities she talks with an echo.

She has startling red lips and a nose to match.

She has such a big nose she could smoke under a shower.

She has such a sour face I'll bet she was raised on a pickle.

She has such a turned-up nose that every time she sneezes she blows her hat off.

She has such bony knees that every time she sits down her knees make a fist.

She has the kind of lips I like—one on top and one on bottom.

She has the same shape as my wallet—flat!

She has to wear dark pink dresses to match her nose.

She has what it takes, only she had it so long nobody wants it.

She hides her age better than a torn-up birth certificate.

She invited me to come and play post office, but I forgot her ZIP code.

She is a bright girl—always lit!

She is a drop-out from driving school. After two lessons they dropped her.

She is a fine girl but,

>her anchor is shifting.
>
>her cargo is dragging.
>
>her joints are swelling.
>
>her nerves are snapping.
>
>her sinuses are clogging.
>
>her skin is wrinkling.
>
>her stomach is growling.

She is a fine girl, but all she ever got was:

>a cold,
>
>a hotfoot,
>
>a sunburn,
>
>a toothache,
>
>angry,
>
>blisters,

confused,

dandruff,

disturbed,

easily tired,

thirsty.

She is a fine talker—the best I ever escaped from.

She is a girl of two words—don't and no.

She is a girl you look at twice. The first time you don't believe it.

She is a girl who accepts rings from strangers. She's a phone operator.

She is a girl:

who cries like a baby.

who drinks like a fish.

who drives like a maniac.

who eats like a horse.

who talks like a parakeet.

who walks like a duck.

She is a girl who has everything. Too bad she has it all in one place.

She is a girl who is:

as exciting as a dunked tea bag.

as fat as a balloon.

as flat as a pancake.

as flat as a pressed flower.

as flat as yesterday's beer.

as flat as a Scotchman's wallet.

as fidgety as an old maid.

as frustrated as a handcuffed opera singer.

as funny as a cry for help.

as helpless as a bride without a can opener.

as helpless as a fat girl in a rumble seat.

as perky as a bubble bath.

as popular as a mouse at a women's club meeting.

as popular as a wet dog in a crowded elevator.

as popular as ants at a picnic.

as popular as poison ivy in a nudist camp.

as sexy as a four-way cold tablet.

as sweet as sugar and twice as lumpy.

as thin as a bookmark.

as thin as a rubber doormat.

as thin as a toothpick.

as thin as wallpaper.

as thirsty as a dry sponge.

as unhappy as a glass blower with hiccups.

as unhappy as a woman with a secret nobody wants to know.

She is a good girl, but she got mixed up with bad company: me.

She is a great driver. Gets 20 miles to a fender.

She is a light eater. As soon as it gets light, she starts eating.

She is a May bride. She may or may not get married.

She is a nodding acquaintance. Every time I meet her, she says: "Nodding doing."

She is a real athlete. Always ready to play ball.

She is a real cowgirl. I always tell her, "You've got a face like a cow, girl!"

She is a real it girl. People look at her and ask, "What is it?"

She is a real oomph girl. When she sits down, the sofa goes oomph.

She is a very strict nudist. Won't even use dressing on her salad.

She is a window dresser. Never pulls the shade down.

She is always a sight to be held.

She is always after a husband and she doesn't care whose.

She is always forgetting—for getting this and for getting that.

She is always one of three things: hungry, thirsty or both.

She is an outdoor girl. Nobody lets her inside.

She is at the age when:

She is too young for boys and too old for toys.

She is too young for Bunny and too old for Brownie.

She is too young for cocktails and too old for pigtails.

She is too young for embraces and too old for braces.

She is too young for Medicare and too old for men to care.

She is too young for mink and too old to scream.

She is too young for wolves and too old for teddy bears.

She is too young for wrinkles and too old for pimples.

She is too young to argue and too old to be spanked.

She is too young to count on her legs and too old to count on her fingers.

She is too young to do housework and too old to do homework.

She is too young to leave home and too old to stay in her crib.

She is too young to say something sensible and too old to say something cute.

She is built like the First National Bank. Everything is deposited in the right places.

She is constantly collecting ills and pills and getting chills.

She is 40 but marked down to 32.

She is interested in a balanced diet. Our food bill always equals my pay check.

She is just like ice cream—sweet and cold!

She is just my type—a girl!

She is listed in **Who's Who**, but doesn't know what's what.

She is my sugar and has the bags to prove it.

She is not a pick-up. She is a let-down.

She is not good at counting calories and has the figure to prove it.

She is not pretty and she is not ugly. She is pretty ugly.

She is on a strict diet. Only eats thin spaghetti.

She is now wearing a mini-skirt over her maxi-shape.

She is one of my best friends. I knew her ever since we were the same age.

MY SILLY GIRL

She is one of those sweet, shy, unassuming girls. You know, a real phony.

She is so bashful:

She goes into a closet to change her mind.

She just ordered a bikini with long sleeves.

She won't go near a salad without dressing.

She won't wear a topless apron.

She wouldn't whistle at a taxi.

She is so cold she has arctic circles under her eyes.

She is so dumb:

After a movie she waits at the backdoor for the star.

After she washed her dog she hung him on the clothesline to dry.

All she knows about nitrates is that they're cheaper than day rates.

And nobody could hold a candle to her. She would always blow it out.

And she must be a twin because one person couldn't be so dumb.

And so confused. She doesn't know whether it is Friday or September.

At a ballet she took a front seat to hear better.

At 6 a.m. she strikes a match to see if the sun is up.

By the time she fills out a job application, the job is taken.

Every time she puts two and two together she gets twenty-two.

Every time she washes an ice cube in hot water she can't find it.

Her idea of housekeeping is to sweep the room with a glance.

If anyone said hello to her she'd be stuck for an answer.

If she said what she thought she would be speechless.

If there's an idea in her head it's in solitary confinement.

She always dips her finger in a glass to find out if it is a soft drink.

She always drives with the emergency brake on. In case of an emergency she is prepared.

She always plays bridge with her gloves on so no one can see her hand.

She always turns a deaf ear to a blind date.

She asked how much a pound cake weighs.

She asked me what size tie I wear.

She bought a pool table for her swimming pool.

She bought me a shaving mug for my electric razor.

She called the Fidelity Insurance Company to have her husband's fidelity insured.

She can memorize a hundred phone numbers, but forgets the names that go with them.

She can't even knit her eyebrows.

She can't even tune her radio.

She can't count to 20 without taking her shoes off.

She claims she can't open the piano because the keys are inside.

She couldn't even spell IOU.

She couldn't tell which way an elevator was going if she had two guesses.

She doesn't know how to spell DDT.

She doesn't see anything wrong with the Leaning Tower of Pisa.

She eats ice cream with a knife and fork.

She even gets sick on her day off.

She even gives her goldfish a bath.

She even put salt in her hair to make believe she had dandruff.

She even smiles for X-ray pictures.

She fed her cow money to get rich milk.

She finally had to move from Cincinnati. Couldn't spell it.

She followed a water sprinkler down the street for eight blocks to tell the driver his wagon was leaking.

She goes to a drive-in movie in the daytime.

She goes to a drive-in movie to see the picture.

She got a beautiful calendar watch for Christmas, so she nailed it to the wall.

She had a full bingo card and didn't know what to yell.

She has an hourglass figure but she doesn't know the time of day.

She has to go out of her mind to get an idea.

She had to go to summer school all winter.

She hangs around the UN building because she likes foreign dishes.

She has trouble steering the vacuum cleaner.

She hired an upstairs maid for her ranch house.

She inquired how long she has to work to get the ten-year pin.

She is afraid to drink tea on her coffee break.

She is afraid to eat a TV dinner in front of the radio.

She is always trying to find new ways to be stupid.

She is wondering how Daylight Savings works. "Do you move the clock up or down?"

She joined a Christmas Club to meet some fellows.

She keeps her cold cream in the icebox to keep it cold.

She keeps asking why they killed the Dead Sea.

She keeps her baby on a phonograph because it has an automatic changer.

She keeps wondering why they don't put unbreakable glass in all fire alarms.

She lost her job as an elevator operator because she couldn't remember the route.

She made slipcovers for her waste basket.

She needed a tutor to pass recess.

She needed two years of tutoring before she could qualify as a dropout.

She never uses toothpaste because her teeth aren't loose.

She once tried to throw away a boomerang.

She opened the cellar window to let out the darkness.

She planted a piece of dogwood and expected to get little puppies.

She plays gin rummy with real gin.

She plays hopscotch with real Scotch.

She pulls the shade down when she changes her mind.

She put a cake of ice in front of her safe so burglars would get cold feet.

She put a mirror on her bathroom ceiling so she could watch herself gargle.

She put a mistletoe in her wallet so she could kiss her money goodbye.

She put crackers in her shoes to feed her pigeon toes.

She puts on a bathing suit when she enters a car pool.

She puts on a hunting suit when she sets the mouse trap.

She returned a flute because it was full of holes.

She salutes General Electric every time she opens the refrigerator.

She shortened the electric cord of her toaster to save electricity.

She signs her check with her typewriter.

She sleeps on the edge of her bed so she can drop right off.

She spent her last dollar buying a pocketbook to put it in.

She spent hours looking for phone numbers in her dictionary.

She spent so much money on new luggage, she couldn't afford to go anywhere.

She spent two weeks in a revolving door looking for the doorknob.

She stands on corners and applauds traffic lights.

She started to dig a well when her house caught fire.

She stayed up all night studying for a blood test.

MY SILLY GIRL

She still carries around a nickel as mad money.

She still keeps her 1954 phone book. Claims 1954 was a good year for telephone books.

She stirs her martini with the wrong fork.

She stands in front of a mirror with her eyes closed to see what she looks like when she's asleep.

She stopped the car in the middle of the bridge for a picnic.

She takes her reducing pills with ice cream.

She threw away a case of 20-year-old Scotch because she thought it was stale.

She threw some butter out the window to see the butter fly.

She tightened the clothesline by moving the house.

She took her car out in a rainstorm because it was a driving rain.

She took her nose apart to see what made it run.

She took her watch apart to see what made it tick.

She took the screen off the window to let the flies out.

She tried to blow out an electric bulb.

She tried to buy glasses for her eye tooth.

She tried to color scrambled eggs for Easter.

She tried to find a cheaper post office.

She tried to find the corner stone in a round house.

She tried to knit a sweater with steel wool.

She tried to pay her income tax with Green Stamps.

She tried to rearrange the seats in her car.

She tried to sell ice cubes to a hothouse.

MY SILLY GIRL

She tried to tip the man at the tollbooth.

She tried to untie a pretzel.

She tried to wash Venetian blinds in a washing machine.

She turned out the lights to see how dark it was.

She used a can opener to open her checkbook.

She wanted a new switchboard because hers was full of holes.

She wanted to be a hat check girl in a nudist camp.

She wanted to be a piano player in a marching band.

She wanted to buy an electric toothbrush, but didn't know whether her teeth were AC or DC.

She wanted to buy bread that wouldn't turn black in her toaster.

She wanted to go to a matinee at a drive-in.

She wanted to know the ZIP code for Lincoln's Gettysburg Address.

She wanted to open a hat concession in an orthodox synagogue.

She wanted to take a his-and-her honeymoon.

She was feeding scrap iron to sheep and expected steel wool.

She was fired from the 5 & 10 store. She couldn't remember the prices.

She was flattered when her doctor told her she had acute appendicitis.

She was 16 years old before she could wave goodbye.

She was trying to buy some food for her rocking horse.

She washed the piano because some of the keys were black.

She went looking for a gas leak with a match.

She went on an Easter egg hunt and shot three eggs.

She went on a honeymoon and took some sleeping pills along.

She went out to buy some vacuum for her vacuum cleaner.

She went to a baseball game with a rope to tie the score.

She went to a chain store to buy a chain.

She went to a general store and looked for the general.

She went to a tennis match with a starched collar.

She went to the fountain of knowledge and just gargled.

She went to the zoo to look for Christmas seals.

She won't buy a dictionary until they make it into a movie.

She won't buy Christmas seals because she doesn't know what to feed them.

She won't talk on the phone to anyone who has a cold.

She would like to have her hair dyed back to its true color, but she forgot what it was.

She would look for a wishbone in a soft-boiled egg.

She would walk into an antique shop and ask: "What's new?"

She wrote a postcard that said: "Check enclosed."

The fortune teller read her mind for half price.

The only test she ever passed was the blood test.

The only thing she ever got straight was the seam of her stocking.

The only things she ever made were mistakes and cigarette ashes.

The only thing she ever read was an eye chart.

The only thing she ever took up in school was space.

When her car needed a new muffler she started to knit one.

When her carburetor was flooded she tried to burp it.

When her doctor put her on a light diet she went out to buy some light bulbs.

When her doctor told her she needed a complete change, she changed the doctor.

When her gas leaked, she fixed it herself by not paying the bill.

When her gas pipe leaked she put a pan under it.

When her house caught fire she sent a telegram to the fire department.

When her house caught fire she turned on the faucets in the bathtub.

When her typewriter bell rings she thinks it's time for lunch.

When I asked her if she'd like a shrimp cocktail, she said she didn't care what size it was.

When I asked her to pass the plate, she asked: "Upper or lower?"

When I gave her a five-karat diamond ring she had it bronzed.

When I told her I had dinner on the cuff she dipped my sleeve in the stew.

When I told her something had a double meaning, she didn't understand either.

When I told her to answer the phone, she said: "Hello, phone!"

When she bought a hammer she asked for an instruction sheet.

When she bought a thermometer she asked for a brand name, like Fahrenheit.

When she bought some Swiss cheese she tried to sew up the holes.

When she couldn't afford a darkroom she bought a pair of very dark glasses.

When she forgot to shake her medicine she jumped up and down for ten minutes.

When she got a job as a bank teller she tried to put some curtains on her window.

When she got a job with the Eagle Laundry she thought she would have to wash some eagles.

When she got an orchestra seat for the theater she took along her flute.

When she got her first bathtub she asked for instructions.

When she had insomnia she didn't lose any sleep over it.

When she had no money for the toll she tried to back up on the George Washington Bridge.

When she heard of shortwave reception she went out and bought a midget radio.

When she is alone with her thoughts she is really alone.

When she is shopping she always puts the eggs on the bottom of her bag so that if they break they won't get all over the other food.

When she receives a postcard she tears it open to see what's inside.

When she saw a sign "Murderer wanted!" she applied for the job.

When she saw snow for the first time she thought it was advertising a soap powder.

When she wanted to get back home she tried to make a U-turn in the Lincoln Tunnel.

When she wanted to write 'Happy Birthday' on a cake she couldn't get the cake into her typewriter.

When she was invited to a house-warming she took along some matches.

When she was invited to a shower she brought some soap.

When she worked for a tea company she kept asking for a coffee break.

When someone gave her some steel wool she started to knit a stove.

When we were introduced and I tipped my hat she dropped a quarter in it.

Whenever she gets a cash present, she goes out to exchange it.

Whenever she loses a button she sews up the button hole.

Whenever she walks around the block she gets lost.

She is so dumb she thinks:

A band-aid is a charity for musicians.

A bed jacket is a jacket for the bed.

A blood vessel is some kind of a ship.

A bomb shelter is a shelter for bombs.

A boycott is a male bed.

A bridge party is a party on a bridge.

A brown cow gives chocolate milk.

A butter knife is made from butter.

A buttress is a female goat.

A can opener is a key to jail.

A cartoon is a song the motorman sings.

A courthouse is a house containing tennis courts.

A courtship is a royal boat.

A dark horse is a nightmare.

A dry martini is a drink you have to consume with a spoon.

A finger wave is a hitchhiker's appeal.

A fjord is a Norwegian automobile.

A football coach has four wheels.

A glass house has a brick window.

A head coach is a psychiatrist.

A hemlock is an attachment for a sewing machine.

A house painter is a painter that makes little pictures of houses.

A Lazy Susan is a girl lying on the couch.

A librarian is a bookie.

A matchbook is a book to read.

A matchmaker works in a match factory.

A meadowlark is a party thrown in the country.

A mistletoe is a foot disease.

A mushroom is a place to love.

A myth is a female moth.

A night school is a school for knights.

A nursery is a school for nurses.

A Peeping Tom is a night watchman.

A psychopath is where psychos walk.

A punch bowl is a fight stadium.

A quorum is a place to keep fish.

A saxophone is a sexy telephone.

A short-order cook is an undersized chef.

A skyscraper is a thing that brushes clouds away.

A square meal is a big order of waffles.

A square meal won't fit her round stomach.

A vegetarian is a horse doctor.

A winding staircase has to be wound up every night.

An eggplant is where they manufacture eggs.

An inkling is a baby fountain pen.

An operetta is a switchboard girl.

Oxygen is an eight-sided figure.

Assets are little donkeys.

Beethoven's Fifth is a bottle of whiskey.

Blackmail means a letter of mourning.

Cold cash is money kept in an air-conditioned bank.

Corn flakes are a foot disease.

Evening clothes are pajamas.

Everything you read in the Sunday paper is true.

Flypaper is an airplane ticket.

Fortifications are two twenty-fications.

German measles are only for Germans.

Half-and-half coffee is served half in the cup and half in the saucer.

Hardening of the arteries is a highway project.

Having one husband is monotony.

Hold-up men are swimming instructors.

If she buys black stockings, she doesn't have to wash them.

If she stops her watch, she will save time.

If she would fill her waterbed with beer, she would get a foam mattress.

If she would iron a four-leaf clover, she would be pressing her luck.

If someone is eating dates, he is consuming time.

If you let chickens swim around in hot water, they will lay hard-boiled eggs.

If you keep chickens in a turning cement mixer, they will lay scrambled eggs.

In a small restaurant the portions look bigger.

Kites are made from flypaper.

Marriage is the first step toward divorce.

Raisins are worried grapes.

Scotch tape comes in bottles.

She cannot serve tea on a coffee table.

She gets ahead walking up on a DOWN escalator.

She has to eat her soup with a knife since her fork leaks.

She has to stand on her head to make an upside-down cake.

She must not wear a T-shirt when drinking coffee.

She went deaf because she went to a ballet and couldn't hear a thing.

She will save money by converting her electric blanket to gas.

Snow tires will melt in summer.

Stagnation is a country for men only.

Strawberries are made from real straw.

Syntax is a tax you have to pay for fun.

That cotton candy is 30 percent dacron.

That horse meat is filly mignon.

The Bluebird of Happiness is just another swallow.

The Cha-Cha **was** written by a man who stuttered.

The English Channel is a TV station that features English films.

The Ford Foundation is a kind of girdle.

The four seasons are pepper, salt, vinegar and oil.

The Hong Kong flu is a Chinese chimney.

The Kentucky Derby is a hat.

The organ grinder works for the monkey, because the monkey collects all the money.

The white line in the center is for bicycles.

This restaurant is closed because the sign says: "HOME COOKING."

To get hot milk you have to rub two cows together.

Veronica Lake is a summer resort.

Water polo is played with sea horses.

Western Union is a cowboy fraternity.

When you buy a foreign car you have to understand the language.

When you go to night school you graduate in cap and nightgown.

You can cool a motor by stripping its gears.

You have to make dinner reservations at a hamburger stand.

You have to study to become a moron.

You need artificial water for artificial flowers.

You need special paint to paint the town red.

You need TNT to blow up a photograph.

She is so fat:

But I worship the ground she covers—New York and New Jersey!

Even her shoelaces don't fit.

Every time she falls down she rocks herself to sleep trying to get up.

Every time she sits down on a barstool she has a hangover.

Every time she stands on a street corner she gets a ticket for parking in a fire zone.

Every time she takes a taxi they try to rush her to the maternity ward.

Every time she tries to stand up her heels flatten out.

Every time she turns around she rearranges the furniture.

Every time she wears a red dress she looks like a bow-legged fire engine.

Everything she eats looks good on her.

For Christmas I bought her a stretch couch.

Her chairs had to be made-to-order.

Her insurance agent took a look at her and turned pale.

Her lips are hiding her double chin.

Her parents brought her home from the hospital in a wheelbarrow.

MY SILLY GIRL

Her shadow leaves marks.

Her shadow weighs 42 pounds.

I bought a small Christmas tree and she wore it as a corsage.

I gave her a belt as a present and she wore it as a wristband.

I had to make two trips to put my arms around her.

I've known her now for six years and have never seen all of her.

If she gains another pound she isn't allowed to walk on a one-way street.

If she grew another foot she would look like a piano.

In a taxi she fills the whole back seat.

In her graduation picture she was the front row.

It takes two dimes to weigh her.

No matter where she sits at home she's always near me.

On the beach people pay her to lie in her shade.

She approaches you from all directions at once.

She bought a house coat and it fits the house just as well.

She bought a hula hoop and used it as a belt.

She bought a violin just to have a place to rest her chin.

She bought two mink wraps—one for each chin.

She can answer the front door without leaving the kitchen.

She can sit around a table all by herself.

She eats so much her teeth are tired.

She even put her full-length mirror sideways.

She gets fan mail from elephants.

She goes through a revolving door in two trips.

She got an offer to model cello cases.

She got her own ZIP code.

She had her picture taken and they charged her a group rate.

She had the mumps for two weeks before we knew it.

She had to buy extra-long shoelaces.

She had to put on a girdle to get into a kimono.

She has a profile like a greyhound bus.

She has more chins than a Chinese telephone directory.

She has to enter Madison Square Garden sideways.

She has to have necklaces made to order.

She has to live in a hangar.

She has to pay overweight for her own body.

She has to sleep alone in a double bed.

She has to take a shower in a carwash.

She has to use a shoehorn to get into a housedress.

She has to use two surfboards—one on each foot.

She has to wear license plates on her charm bracelet.

She has trouble going through the Lincoln Tunnel.

She is a population explosion all by herself.

She is in a crowd even when she is alone.

She is living beyond her seams.

She is not only a sight, she is a panorama.

She is running out of places to hide her weight.

She is two inches taller sitting down.

She leaned on a pool table and the legs caved in.

She looks like a bass fiddle.

She looks like a kangaroo with all the kids at home.

She measures five feet in any direction.

She models for duffle bags.

She models for pyramids.

She needs a half a jar of cold cream for each chin.

She needs a six-piece bikini.

She needs two tokens to get into the subway turnstile.

She not only kept her girlish figure, she doubled it.

She outnumbers herself.

She put on a wedding gown and three people went snow-blind.

She sings quartet by herself.

She stepped on a cigarette butt and made a hole in the sidewalk.

She stepped on a scale and it said: One at a time, please!

She takes a shower and her feet don't get wet.

She uses a hammock as a chinstrap.

She uses a tent as a bathing suit.

She was born March 17, 18 and 19.

She was her own buddy in summer camp.

She wears red earrings and looks like the end of a bus.

She wears two girdles—one upper and one lower.

She will eat anything that won't bite first.

She wore a yellow dress and five men yelled: "Taxi! Taxi!"

The Blue Cross charges her group rates.

The only exercise she does is eating.

The only exercise she does is walking to and from the table.

The only exercise she does is with her knife and fork.

The only thing bigger than her stomach is her appetite.

The only thing she ever took off was two weeks vacation.

They always ask her to take the freight elevator.

They don't measure her for a dress. They survey her.

They used her many times as a roadblock.

To take her picture you need two cameras.

We call her the little plumpkin.

When a bus hit her by accident the bus was damaged.

When her doctor put her on a seven-day diet she ate the whole thing at one meal.

When her husband carried her over the threshold he had to make two trips.

When she blew a kiss the whole house shook.

When she boarded a boat it became a submarine.

When she dances in a nightclub she needs the whole floor.

When she eats lobster she needs two bibs.

When she entered a Miss America contest they thought she represented two states.

When she enters an empty bus she fills up half of it.

When she rides in a plane she gets three seats.

When she set foot on a ferry it sank.

When she stepped into a Volkswagen all four tires went flat.

When she stepped on a ship it tilted.

When she turned around in a supermarket she knocked down five shelves.

When she walked down the aisle with her groom they had to walk single file.

When she walked over the Brooklyn Bridge she stopped all traffic.

When she walked through Grand Central Station she blocked every track entrance.

When she walks in the rain she needs two umbrellas.

When she walks the street at night it looks like a mob.

When she wears a red dress she looks like a high-rise fire hydrant.

When she wants to use a public phone booth she has to stand outside.

When she weighs herself she doesn't tip the scale. She bribes it.

You would run out of gas driving around her.

She is so good looking, men take one look at her and shoot their wives.

She is so homely:

A Peeping Tom reached into her window and pulled down the shade.

After she used a mudpack she looked nice, then it fell off.

All a sweater did for her was make her itch.

As a child they gave her a sandbox filled with quicksand.

As a nurse they kept her in the operating room so she always wore a mask.

At her wedding everybody kissed the groom.

At restaurants she is never allowed to sit near the windows.

At the Christmas party they hung her picture and kissed the mistletoe.

Boys kiss the ground she walks on. It's better than kissing her.

But, for an ugly girl she isn't bad looking.

But, she is a very neat girl—not one wrinkle out of place.

Even at a charity ball the fellows won't ask her for a dance.

Even garlic backs away from her.

Even the Welcome Wagon wouldn't stop at her door.

Even when she looks good she looks terrible.

Even when she worked in a department store basement she was no bargain.

Every time she goes near a bank the alarm goes off.

Every time she goes to a zoo she scares the animals.

From the back she looks like a celebrity and from the front like a calamity.

Her appendix was taken out more times than she was.

Her complexion is mostly seasick green.

Her dad took off the brakes on her baby carriage.

Her face looks better from the back.

Her face not only stops a clock, it even stops her phone.

MY SILLY GIRL

Her mother used to diaper her face.

Her phone doesn't even ring when she is in the shower.

Her psychiatrist makes her lie face down on his couch.

I think she looks much better with all the curlers in her hair.

I took a polaroid picture of her and the camera refused to develop it.

I wouldn't kiss her with a set of borrowed lips.

If it weren't for goose pimples, she wouldn't have a figure at all.

If she were a building, she'd be condemned.

In a bathing suit she looks like a potato with legs.

In her family album they keep only the negatives.

In the morning, without make-up, she looks like a preview of a horror show.

It's all right to be ugly, but she overdoes it.

Kissing her is like scratching a place that doesn't itch.

Last year she won the Ugly contest.

On her honeymoon the groom asked for separate rooms in the hotel.

Once, when she got on a bus, the driver quit.

She always gets a seat on the subway. When people look at her they get up and walk to the next car.

She always has to dance by herself.

She always wears tight shoes. That's the only time she ever gets squeezed.

She bought a new gown that's strapless, hipless and hopeless.

She bought a love seat ten years ago and half of it is still new.

She calls herself a straight actress. Her measurements are 36—36—36.

She can meet all her friends in a phone booth.

She can go out only on Halloween. It's the only time people won't stare at her.

She comes home with the same lipstick she started out with.

She could collect insurance without having an accident.

She couldn't lure you out of a burning building.

She even makes coffee nervous.

She even has freckles on her teeth.

She goes every week to an optometrist just to have somebody look into her eyes.

She goes to a beauty parlor on Monday and comes back on Wednesday.

She has all the curves a girl should have, only on her they look like corners.

She had a coming-out party, but they made her go back in.

She had her face lifted so many times, it's out of focus.

She has a steady date at the beauty parlor, daily from 8 to 10.

She has a sympathetic face. It has everybody's sympathy.

She has been turned down more often than a bedspread.

She has hips like a beach umbrella.

She has that certain far-away look. The further away, the better she looks.

She has teeth like sparkling water—one down and seven up.

She has to play one-handed Ping-Pong.

She is a perfect model—for ship builders.

She joined a key club and they changed all the locks.

She just bought a reversible coat. What she really needs is a reversible face!

She keeps reading the want ads, but nobody wants her.

She looks better with a gas mask on her face.

She looks good in anything but the mirror.

She looks like a dollar bill—thin, flat, green and wrinkled.

She looks like a lost weekend.

She looks like a million, but nobody can be that old.

She looks like a passport picture of a prune.

She looks like a professional blind date.

She looks like a Sunday ice cream on Monday morning.

She looks like a tea bag after it was dipped 12 times.

She looks like a well-kept grave.

She looks like an elephant trying to forget.

She looks like an unmade bed.

She needs so much make-up, they made her join the painter's union.

She never will be as old as she looks.

She only gets kissed in blackouts.

She puts cold cream on her face and it curdles.

She rents herself out for Halloween parties.

She should have lived in the Dark Ages. She looks terrible in the light.

She sleeps with her face to the pillow so she won't scare burglars.

She spends hours at the beauty parlor just for estimates.

She thinks she's a siren, but she looks more like a false alarm.

She tries to look like a dream, but she looks more like a nightmare.

She used to be a model in Alaska. Posed for totem poles.

She was a wallflower at every party. Now they won't even let her in.

She was thrown out of a dance for loitering.

She wears her hair over her shoulder. She should wear it over her face.

She went to the beauty parlor four times last week and it didn't help much.

She won first prize at a masquerade party without wearing a mask.

She wore see-through blouses but nobody wanted to.

The Board of Health wanted to close her face.

The boys don't call her attractive; in fact, nobody ever calls her.

The doctor refused to sign her birth certificate.

The lifeguard would rescue her only on slow days.

The mosquitoes bite her with closed eyes.

The only charm she has is on her bracelet.

The only man she ever had at her feet was a chiropodist.

The only person who ever asked her to get married was her mother.

The only place she is ever invited to is outside.

The only ring she ever got was over the phone.

The only thing female about her is her name.

The only thing flatter than her voice is her figure.

The only things she has in her hope chest are moth balls.

The only thing that can make her look good is distance.

The only time she gets squeezed is when she wears a girdle.

The Red Cross wanted her to pose for disaster pictures.

The Welcome Wagon made a detour around her house.

They copied the features of her face for Halloween masks.

They couldn't lift her face so they lowered her body.

Though it's all right to be ugly, she abuses the privilege.

Though she has a winning smile, she has a losing face.

Though she has an hourglass figure, it is later than she thinks.

We had to buy her back from the dogcatcher eight times.

What a figure! I have seen better legs on kitchen tables.

When her boyfriend takes her out for supper he always sits beside her.

When she ate at the captain's table on a cruise, he lost his appetite.

When she bought a dog, he ran away from her.

When she entered a beauty contest they fined her $50.

When she entered the Miss America contest they took away her citizenship.

When she fell out of a bus, the driver was given a ticket for littering.

When she leaves the beauty parlor they ask her to use the backdoor.

When she moved in she was fired upon by the Welcome Wagon.

When she peels onions, the onions cry.

When she walks along the pier even the tugboats stop whistling.

When she walks into a room all the mice jump up on the chairs.

When she was born the doctor spanked her mother.

When she was born they didn't know whether to buy a crib or a cage.

When she was the only person to enter a beauty contest, she won second prize.

When she went to a wax museum they started to dust her off.

When she went to the beach the tide went out and never came back.

When she won a medal even a French general refused to kiss her.

When the boss chases her around the desk, he limps.

When they played hide-and-seek nobody looked for her.

Whenever she drops a handkerchief, she has to pick it up herself.

Whenever she goes to the zoo, she needs two tickets—one for going in and one for getting out.

Whenever we go out, I take a taxi. I hate to be seen with her on the street.

Where other girls have curves she has detours.

While I was walking with her, a policeman stopped me and asked if I already reported the accident.

Some girls have curves. She has U-turns.

Sometimes she turns on the teakettle, just to hear a whistle.

She is so hungry she eats a cake while it's baking.

She is so hungry, she eats like a baby sitter.

She is so lazy, even her dishes are drip-dry.

She is so modest, she blindfolds herself while taking a bath.

She is so modest, she wouldn't go near her car when told that the gears were stripped.

She is so old:

Even her hot flashes are lukewarm.

Her age is her business, but she never talks about business.

Her age is her own business, but in her case she's practically out of business.

Her birthday cake has been declared a fire hazard.

Her last birthday cake looked like a prairie fire.

Her real age is the only secret she would keep.

Her Social Security number is 4.

Her teeth are the only things she has that aren't wrinkled.

It took her 10 minutes to blow out all her candles on her last birthday.

No wine could be older than she is.

On her last birthday she had enough candles to give everybody a suntan.

On her last birthday the candles melted the cake.

On my slice of her birthday cake were 12 candles.

She admits approaching 30. I wonder from which direction.

She could be the wife of the captain of the Mayflower.

She doesn't celebrate birthdays anymore. She just knocks on wood.

She doesn't learn history. She remembers it.

She feels on Friday like she used to feel on Monday morning.

She gets estimates from undertakers.

She gets winded playing checkers.

She gets winded watching television.

She had a bonfire in the center of her birthday cake.

She had a driver's license for covered wagons.

She had the lemon concession at the Boston Tea Party.

She has enough wrinkles in her face to hold a two-day rain.

She has more wrinkles on her face than a parchment.

MY SILLY GIRL

She has more wrinkles than a pound of prunes.

She has more wrinkles than a roadmap.

She has to celebrate her birthday outdoors, because the candles would set off the smoke detector.

She needs a fire permit to light candles on her birthday cake.

She needs two cakes to hold all her birthday candles.

She pays more for the candles than for her birthday cake.

She put so many candles on her cake she barbecued the ceiling.

She remembers Howard Johnson when he only had three flavors.

She remembers Madam Butterfly when she was a caterpillar.

She remembers the Telephone Company being called: "American Smoke Signal Company."

She remembers when Heinz had only three varieties.

She stepped into an antique shop and someone tried to buy her.

She was born in the year only the Lord knows.

She will never be as old as she looks.

The last time she lit all her candles she needed 10 matches.

The only time she will see 60 again is on a speed limit sign.

When I asked her to pass the salt and the pepper she had to make two trips.

When I tried to count her birthday candles the heat drove me back.

When she lit all her candles three people collapsed from the heat.

Whenever someone asks her for her real age she only tells half of it.

She is so popular, her phone even rings when it's off the hook.

She is so popular, she even has her phone number in the Yellow Pages.

She is so popular, she gets more phone calls than a bookie.

She is so popular, she gets more phone calls than the AAA on a snowy night.

She is so rich, she has a mink lining in her sable coat.

She is so thin:

A backache and a stomachache would hit her in the same place.

Every time she swallows a raisin her stomach sticks out.

From a side view she looks like a record.

Her husband slipped her wedding ring over her head.

Her shadow weighs more than she does.

I have seen more meat in a ten-cent hamburger.

I've thrown away soup bones with more meat on them.

If she didn't have warts her strapless dress wouldn't stay up.

If she wore a peekaboo dress, it would be a false alarm.

If you see a door open and nothing comes in, that's her!

It takes two of her to make a shadow.

She can look through a keyhole with both eyes.

She can stand on a bag of potato chips without crunching any.

She could have only one measle at a time.

She could model thermometers.

She could play the piano from the inside.

She could tap dance on a chocolate eclair.

She could walk through a harp without hitting a note.

She could wear a striped dress with only one stripe.

She could weigh herself on a postage scale.

She doesn't even cast a shadow in bright sunshine.

She eats garlic just to prove she's breathing.

She has a profile like a bookmark.

She has a truly vegetarian figure—no meat.

She has muscles like potatoes—mashed potatoes.

She has the word FRONT tattooed on her chest.

She has to inhale to throw a shadow.

She holds her hands over her head and she looks like a fork.

She looks like a broom with clothes on.

She looks like a hockey stick.

She looks like a totem pole that came to life.

She looks like Melba toast.

She looks like six o'clock—up and down.

She made herself a dress from my old necktie.

MY SILLY GIRL

She modeled for ironing boards.

She needs only one earring.

She needs suspenders to hold up her girdle.

She once swallowed an olive and eight men left town.

She reminds me of a roll of film—underdeveloped.

She stood sideways in school and was marked absent.

She swallowed a cherry pit and everybody thought she was expecting.

She sways in the breeze of an electric fan.

She tied knots in her stockings to make it look like knees.

She told me she's a showgirl, but she doesn't have anything to show.

She took a bath and almost slipped down the drain.

She used to model bicycle pumps.

She uses her legs as knitting needles.

She yawns and her dress falls down.

There is more meat on a butcher's apron.

When her chest itches she has to scratch her back.

When her date took her to a restaurant he was told to check the umbrella.

When I take her home I just slip her under the door.

When she closes one eye she looks like a needle.

When she drinks tomato juice she looks like a thermometer.

When she forgets the key she gets into the house through the keyhole.

When she gets into a taxi they leave the vacant sign up.

When she puts on a fur coat she looks like a pipe cleaner.

When she sits on a dime six cents are still showing.

When she stands sideways she looks like wallpaper.

When she steps on a scale it doesn't move.

When she takes off her clothes she looks like the unveiling of a golf stick.

When she wears a green dress she looks like asparagus.

When she wears a red dress she looks like a firecracker.

When she wears a yellow dress she looks like a pencil.

When she wears her hair straight down she looks like a mop.

Whenever she carries a handbag she is off balance.

You have to look at her twice to see her once.

She is the kind of a girl who wants the moon, the stars and the sun. So I took her to the planetarium.

She is the kind of a woman that talks endlessly about things that leave her speechless.

She is the most respected girl in town. She is also the loneliest.

She is the picture of her father and the sound track of her mother.

She is 29 going on indefinitely.

She is very easy on the eyes but hard on the wallets.

She is very handy around the kitchen. And so is a garbage can.

She is very loyal. Years ago she reached an age she liked and she stuck to it.

She is very temperamental. Eighty percent temper and the rest mental.

She is wearing one of those hats that looks like there was no mirror in the hat shop.

She just saved me a lot of money. She married someone else.

She kept playing two transistor radios in her ears and got a stereophonic headache.

She kept saying she wanted her children young. "Who wants old children?"

She knew she was going to get married a few times so she bought a washable wedding dress.

She knows all the answers but nobody asks her the questions.

She looks as good as an income tax refund.

She looks good in anything but a mirror.

She looks like a doll. Even her hair is pasted on.

She looks like a million—like a million other girls.

She makes a living holding hands. She's a manicurist.

She married a plumber and now she is sitting pretty.

She may be English, but the look in her eyes is international.

She may not always be right, but she is never wrong.

She may not be able to add, but she certainly can distract.

She met the most wonderful man. It was a case of wink, blink and mink.

She must use gunpowder on her face. It always looks shot.

She never cleans house. She only moves the dust around.

She never forgot her age—once she decided what it was to be.

She only wears short nightgowns because she doesn't sleep very long.

She really has an unusual voice. It's like asthma set to music.

She really sends me and when I get back she is usually gone.

She reduces and reduces but never becomes a bargain.

She saved all her kisses for all her life and with the first man she lost her life savings.

She says her age is 35. I think that's her blood pressure.

She says she is 33 but there are very few people alive to contradict her.

She said she would do anything for a mink coat and now she can't button it.

She shops like a human dynamo—charges everything!

She sings with heart and soul. She should try it with a voice sometime.

She speaks loose talk with forked tongue.

She still has a parking problem with her car. It is how and not where.

She sure has big ears. From the front she looks like a taxi with both doors open.

She swears she's never been kissed. She can hardly be blamed for swearing.

She talked so much her tongue got sunburned.

She talks so much, that every month she has to go and get her tonsils retreaded.

She thinks a thing of beauty is a boy forever.

She thinks her chin is her best feature. It looks more like a double feature.

She took after her mother who took after her father who took after the maid.

She took it so hard when she reached 40 that she bounced right back to 35.

She used to be a dreamboat but now her anchor drags and her cargo shifted.

She used to sing with a band but now she wears a little more.

She uses too many four-letter words, like: Don't! Can't! Won't!

She waited so long for her dreamboat to come in her pier collapsed.

She walks slowly but her stockings are running.

She walks with a stoop and wants to marry him.

She wanted a simple hair dryer so I moved her chair closer to the oven.

She wanted a white wedding so she prayed for snow.

She wanted to be a bubble dancer but her Dad said no soap!

She wanted to buy a low cut dress but the store wouldn't cut the price any lower.

She wanted to marry a big movie star or nothing. And she got her wish. Married a big nothing.

She was at the stage where she wouldn't even reveal the age she used to say she was.

She was drinking so much alcohol, I was afraid to let her smoke.

She was going to get a divorce until she realized that all her dresses zipped down her back.

She was indeed a sight to be held.

She was my blind date, but sure opened my eyes.

She was one of those girls who have seen better nights.

She was out shopping all day, but the only thing she got was a headache.

She was pure as snow, but how she could drift.

She was quite a success as a bubble dancer until her career blew up in her face.

She was so bowlegged:

> She could get out of a car on both sides at the same time.
>
> She could walk down a bowling alley during the game.
>
> She looked like a bite out of a doughnut.
>
> We used to hang her over the door for good luck.

She was so embarrassed she tripped over the roses in the rug.

She was so sentimental she wanted to get married in her Grandma's dress. She looked lovely, but her Grandma froze to death.

She was so short her mini-skirt dragged on the floor.

She was the kind of a girl you'd like to bring home to Mother, if you could trust Father.

She was the kind of outdoor girl you wanted to take indoors.

She was told she had a nice profile. Now she's trying to walk sideways.

She was 21 the same time I was. I don't know how old she is now.

She was wearing a sweater so tight, I could hardly breathe.

She wears a sweater to accentuate the positive, and a girdle to eliminate the negative.

She wears the kind of a dress that keeps everyone warm but her.

She went on a steak diet and the first week lost $25.

She will go anyplace for exercise as long as she doesn't have to walk.

She will lose her temper, but never her appetite.

She will never give away a secret, but she will exchange it for another.

She works as a draftsman. Every time I make plans she draws the line.

My
Wife
and
I

Arguing with my wife is like blowing out a light bulb.

Before we got married she played hard to get, now she plays hard to keep.

Every man needs a wife because too many things go wrong you can't blame on the government.

For twenty-five years I have been in love with the same woman. If my wife ever finds out she'll kill me.

I always give my wife her present on December 15. That way she can exchange it in time for Christmas.

I always like to talk about my wife's cooking. Talk about it, yes, but eating it is another story.

I always say, be kind to your wife and she may help you with the dishes.

I always take her to the best restaurants. Someday I'll take her inside.

I always tell my wife the truth, even if I have to lie a little.

I always tell my wife who's the boss. I step right up and say: "You're the boss!"

I'm a married man and I can't ask for a better wife, but I would like to.

I'm always careful not to drop my wife's cakes. They might break my foot.

I'm always kidding about my wife. But every time I introduce her to anybody they say: "You must be kidding!"

I'm having trouble with my wife. When I'm at the office I can't get her on the phone and when I'm home I can't get her off the phone.

I'm lucky. I have a wife and a cigarette lighter and both are working.

I'm not saying my wife's a lousy housewife, but she keeps clogging up the dishwasher with paper plates.

I'm not saying she is a bad cook, but my doctor advised me to eat out more often.

I bought my wife one of those paper dresses but she returned it, complaining the headlines were three days old.

I can't get along with my wife—she understands me!

I claim two exemptions for my wife because she has a split personality.

I don't drink to my wife. I drink because of her.

I don't have to tell my wife anything. My neighbors do it for me.

I don't know if my wife has the measles or the mumps. But I'll know tomorrow. She'll either break out or shut up.

I don't know what I'd do without my wife. She'll never let me find out.

MY WIFE AND I

I don't know where my money is coming from, but my wife sure knows where it is going.

I don't mind that my wife always has the last word. It's the waiting for it that I hate.

I drive my wife crazy. I smile in my sleep.

I earn four dollars an hour and my wife spends six dollars a minute.

I figured out a way to cut down my wife's expenses. I took away all her credit cards.

I finally broke my wife's habit of biting her nails. I hid her teeth.

I finally found the perfect way to avoid dishpan hands. I let my wife do the dishes.

I finally found the most wonderful woman. The only trouble is her husband wants her back.

I gave her a bridge-lamp for her birthday but she made me put it back on the bridge.

I gave her a present that made her so excited she could hardly wait to exchange it.

I gave her an X-ray of my chest for Christmas. Just wanted to show her that my heart was in the right place.

I gave my wife a $100 gift certificate for her birthday. She used it as a down payment for a $5000 bracelet.

I get two vacations a year. When my boss goes to Europe and when my wife goes to Florida.

I got this dog for my wife. I wish I could make a trade like that every day.

I have a big problem. If I ever meet the girl of my dreams, what will I do with my wife?

I have a dear wife. She cost me a fortune.

I have a real problem with my wife. She watches TV all day and has no time to do any cooking.

I have antique furniture and a wife to match.

I have been up all night nursing a grouch. My wife is sick.

I have got the best wife in the country. Sometimes I wish she'd stay there.

I have had bad luck with both my wives. The first divorced me and the second won't.

I have never thought about divorce—murder yes, but not divorce.

I haven't spoken to my wife in years. I didn't want to interrupt her.

I hid my wife's Christmas present in the broom closet. That's one door she never opens.

I just hired three helping hands for my wife: a dumb waiter, a Lazy Susan, and a silent butler.

I keep telling my wife I couldn't live without her. And I sure couldn't. She's the one who is working.

I knew I was in trouble the minute I got married. My wife's parents sent me a thank-you note.

I love to dance with strangers and nobody dances stranger than my wife.

I mailed her a birthday cake air-mail and I hope she gets it while the candles are still burning.

I married my wife for money and believe me, I earned it.

I met my wife at a dance. I thought she was home with the kids.

I met my wife at a travel office. She was looking for a vacation and I was the last resort.

I met my wife on a bus. Oh, why didn't I take a taxi home that night?

I miss my wife a lot. She's quick at dodging.

I never argue with my wife. I might win and then I would be in real trouble.

I never expect to find the perfect wife, but it's lots of fun looking.

I never knew what happiness meant until I got married—then it was too late.

I once advertised for a wife and 100 husbands offered me theirs.

I promised my wife I will cut down on my drinking if she cuts down on her cooking.

I remember when and where I got married, but what escapes me is why.

I sent my wife to the seashore for a holiday and what a holiday I had!

I speak several languages, but I can't master the tongue of my wife.

I spent New Year's Eve with one of the biggest spenders—my wife.

I sure know how to handle a wife, but my wife won't let me.

I take my wife out every night but she always finds her way back.

I think my marriage is insecure. We are married now five years and my wife still gives me the guest towels.

I think my wife is Irish. Every time I eat her cooking I turn green.

I told my wife many times: "I like your mother-in-law better than mine."

I took my wife out for a seven-course dinner. A six-layer cake and coffee.

I took my wife to see a movie. It was the longest time we've spent together since our honeymoon.

I used to go out with a perfect 36 until my wife came in with a loaded 45.

I wake up every morning with a nagging headache—my wife.

I wanted to buy her a pair of Capri pants, but I didn't know the size of her capri.

I wanted to buy my wife some flowers to match her eyes but I couldn't find bloodshot carnations.

I wanted to get her a corsage, but I didn't know what size she wore.

I was going to buy her some handkerchiefs, but I forgot the size of her nose.

I was taking shots for my cold, but my wife took my bottle away.

I was trying to get a new car for my wife, but nobody would swap.

I was wrong when I admired her chin. She started to raise two more.

I went all over town to get something for my wife, but I didn't get a single offer.

I'll never forget our wedding. I've tried, but my wife won't let me.

I won my wife at a quiz show. I didn't know the truth and she was the consequence.

I won't say my wife is fussy but she exchanges gift certificates.

I would enjoy family life if it weren't for two things: my wife and my children.

I would have a great marriage if my wife would defrost as fast as her TV-dinners.

I would like to buy some flowers for the woman I love, but my wife won't let me.

MY WIFE AND I

I would never buy an encyclopedia; my wife knows everything.

I wouldn't say my wife talks a lot, but I had laryngitis for two weeks and she didn't notice it.

I wouldn't worry about my wife wearing her dresses a little shorter if she'd only wear them a little longer.

If it weren't for my wife I wouldn't be what I am today—broke!

It's amazing what my wife would rather have than money.

Many times my wife has put her foot down—right on my toes.

Married life is great! It's my wife I can't stand.

Money means nothing to my wife, so she spends it to get rid of it.

My best friend ran away with my wife, and let me tell you, I miss him.

My doctor advised me to lose annoying weight, but my wife won't divorce me.

My eyes were never good and I have a wife to prove it.

One way to put my wife in good humor is to do the dishes for her.

Our room is so small, every time I cross my legs, I kick my wife.

Since I got married I don't worry about bad breath. I never get a chance to open my mouth in front of my wife.

Since my wife is brushing her teeth with gunpowder, she's been shooting off her mouth again.

Sure my wife makes money—disappear!

The best way to get my wife to change her mind is to agree with her.

The only chance I get to open my mouth around my wife is when I yawn.

The only kinds of books she likes are checkbooks.

The only time my wife pays strict attention to what I say is when I'm asleep.

Then one night my wife made a big mistake. She threw a boomerang at me.

There are only three things my wife can't control: her temper, her weight and her children.

There are three things my wife can make out of nothing: a hat, a salad and a quarrel.

There isn't another woman in the world like my wife— thank God!

There's nothing wrong with my wife that a miracle won't cure.

There's only one thing that keeps me from being a happily married man—my wife!

We didn't know what to do about our house so we divided it 50:50. She took the inside and I took the outside.

We had a power failure in our house. My wife lost her voice.

We never go out. I sit at the TV set and smoke and my wife sits beside me and fumes.

Whenever my wife waxes the floor, I get a bottle and polish it off.

When I come home late my wife hits the ceiling. She's a poor shot.

When I first met her I called her dear. Now she's more expensive.

When I talk my wife listens: to the radio, TV, record player....

When my wife complained that to clean the house almost kills her, I went and bought a bigger house.

When my wife goes shopping she comes home with everything but money.

When my wife goes to the supermarket she never has shelf-control.

Whenever my wife goes on a diet all she loses is her sense of humor.

When my wife says she is dreaming of a white Christmas she means ermine or white mink.

When my wife went away for good she took everything but the children.

My Wife

My wife always knows when it's payday. I've got to hand it to her.

My wife always lets me have the first word in any argument.

My wife always makes trouble. As soon as she saw me kissing my secretary she went and told the maid.

My wife always misses her afternoon nap. She sleeps right through it.

My wife begged me: "Be an angel and let me drive!" So I let her drive and now she's an angel.

My wife believes in sharing our money. She shares my paycheck with Saks, Gimbels and Lord & Taylor.

My wife belongs in a zoo: She dresses like a peacock, sings like a nightingale, acts like a lovebird and works like a horse.

My wife bought a dress marked 'Half-off!' And that's the way she wore it.

My wife bought a very useful hat. When she's not wearing it, I clean the car with it.

My wife bought me an electric typewriter. Now she is out shopping for a chair to match.

MY WIFE AND I

My wife bought me some bloodshot socks to match my eyes.

My wife bought three cocktail dresses and she doesn't even drink.

My wife brings more bills into the house than a Congressman.

My wife brought home a big surprise. She bought a hat that really looks like a hat.

My wife buys everything on time. We have payments coming out of our years.

My wife calls me 'Darling' twice a year—before her birthday and before Christmas.

My wife calls our checking account the 'Shrinking Fund.'

My wife came home all wet from a drive-in carwash. She forgot to take the car.

My wife can keep a secret, but only one at a time!

My wife can keep a secret with telling effect.

My wife can say more in a look than I can say in a book.

My wife can sure keep a secret. We were engaged three months before I found out about it.

My wife can't play golf. She doesn't even know how to hold a caddy.

My wife cleans our house weekly—very weakly!

My wife convinced me that we needed a new car. She wrecked the old one.

My wife defrosted so many TV dinners, now she thinks she has experience in show business.

My wife didn't wear her new hat at the Easter parade. She carried it on a long stick to make sure everybody noticed it.

MY WIFE AND I

My wife diets on any kind of food she can lay her hands on.

My wife does less shopping, but she spends more.

My wife does my laundry just fine. Every shirt comes out dazzling white, even the blue ones.

My wife doesn't care what my secretary looks like, just as long as he is efficient.

My wife doesn't lie about her age. She just claims she's as old as I am. And then she lies about my age.

My wife doesn't mind Christmas shopping. She charges right ahead.

My wife doesn't want me to remember her birthday and is disappointed when I forget it.

My wife dresses in the new look. But it doesn't help much, she is using the old parts.

My wife drives like lightning—always striking trees.

My wife even hired an interior decorator to do the closets.

My wife failed five driving tests. But she isn't quitting, her instructor is.

My wife fell into a wishing well. I didn't know those things worked.

My wife finally worked out our budget. But one of us has to stop eating.

My wife found a new investment. She puts all her money into trading stamps.

My wife found a new way to save money. She uses mine.

My wife found a real bargain in the supermarket. The regular 45-cent can was reduced from 85 to 77 cents.

My wife gave me a present that made my eyes pop out—a shirt with a size 12 collar.

My wife gave me a wonderful birthday present. She let me win an argument.

My wife gave me the best years of her life. At her age she should be glad to get rid of them.

My wife gets gray worrying over her gray hair.

My wife gets so emotional. She read that some foundations were being investigated. So, she hid her girdle.

My wife got a ticket for speeding and she was just changing a tire at the time.

My wife got three tickets during her driving lesson.

My wife had a fight with her mother. Now she's going home to my mother.

My wife had a typical shopping day. She came home with an empty wallet, three pages of trading stamps and two parking tickets.

My wife has a bad habit. She takes my race track money and blows it on the rent.

My wife has a great desirability. She desires more than anyone I know.

My wife has a great sense of balance, except in her checkbook.

My wife has a long-playing tongue.

My wife has a mini-skirt, a mini-car and a mini-poodle. So why does she have a big mouth?

My wife has a strange way of getting even with the phone company. She knocks down their poles with her car.

My wife has a tongue like a poison arrow.

My wife has a wonderful way to make a long story short. She interrupts.

My wife has an impediment in her speech. Every once in a while she stops to breathe.

MY WIFE AND I

My wife has an impediment in her speech. She can't stop talking.

My wife has been missing for four days. I don't know whether she left me or went shopping.

My wife has been stopped so often by traffic cops that they finally gave her a season ticket.

My wife has green lips from kissing money goodbye.

My wife has her way with money. The trouble is, it's her way and my money.

My wife hasn't spoken to me for two weeks. She says I had no right to paste travel posters on the walls of her mother's bedroom.

My wife hasn't talked to me for three days. I have to get her something to show my appreciation.

My wife has sinus trouble, she always says: "Sinus a check for this, sinus a check for that."

My wife has so many dresses in her closets that are too good to throw away, but not good enough to wear.

My wife has the fastest gums in the East.

My wife has two closets full of nothing to wear.

My wife hired a cleaning woman who comes in twice a week. But the only thing she ever cleaned out was the refrigerator.

My wife is a can-can girl. Can I have this? Can I have that?

My wife is a careful driver. Always drives on the sidewalk just to avoid traffic.

My wife is a great shopper. One day she took sick and two stores went out of business.

My wife is a magician. She can turn anything into an argument.

My wife is a meticulous eater. Even uses a knife and fork to eat potato chips.

MY WIFE AND I

My wife is a regular clothes-horse. When she wears certain clothes she looks like a horse.

My wife is a vegetarian. Every time I get home she asks: "Where is the cabbage?"

My wife is a weight-watcher. She just sits and watches her weight.

My wife is able to drive the wrong way on a two-way street.

My wife is all tired out. She spent all day changing her mind.

My wife is always giving me sentimental things. Like on Easter she gave me a rabbit punch.

My wife is always losing something. She even lost her shoes in a drive-in.

My wife is always talking to herself. The worst part is, she thinks I'm listening.

My wife is an after-dinner speaker. And before and during.

My wife is an excellent driver. She only has trouble with starting, stopping, turning and parking.

My wife is away and the whole house seems empty. Except the sink, that's full of dishes.

My wife is a blonde, a brunette and a redhead. The wig store had a sale.

My wife is crazy about door-to-door peddlers. We own everything in the world that cost a dollar a week.

My wife is even-tempered—mad all the time.

My wife is money crazy. I don't give her any and she goes crazy.

My wife is never going out to work. Unless she wants food, clothes, and a place to sleep.

My wife is not talking to me since I patched a tire with one of her pancakes.

MY WIFE AND I

My wife is now at the awkward age. She no longer remembers her age.

My wife is now on one of those seafood diets. She can see food but can't eat it.

My wife is now 60. I'll split two for one and get two 30's.

My wife is now on an economy kick. Every time I try to economize, she kicks.

My wife is overweight and she blamed Noah. Every time she sits down to eat she takes two of everything.

My wife is reading a mystery book—her collection of cooking recipes.

My wife is so busy cooking for me, she never has time to run out to get a sandwich for herself.

My wife is so fussy. She cleans the garbage before throwing it away.

My wife is so neat. I get up at four in the morning for a glass of water and when I get back my bed is made.

My wife is so neat. She covers everything with plastic. Our house looks like we are expecting rain.

My wife is so neat, when it rains we have wall-to-wall newspapers on the floor.

My wife is so sensitive. She cries when a traffic light is against her.

My wife is studying to drive and I'm studying First Aid.

My wife is such a bore, I don't even listen when she talks in her sleep.

My wife is suing for divorce and she's asking for custody of the money.

My wife is the demure type. Demure I give her, demure she wants.

My wife is the kind of a housewife who always puts off today what the maid can do tomorrow.

MY WIFE AND I

My wife is the salt of the earth. I've been trying to shake her for years.

My wife is trying hard to keep a clean house. But yesterday the phone rang and she couldn't find it.

My wife is unpredictable. I never know why I'm going to be wrong about what and when.

My wife is very careful about money. She spends it fast so she won't lose it.

My wife is very punctual; in fact, she buys everything on time.

My wife is willing to live on my income if I get another for myself.

My wife is willing to share everything with me, except her clothes closet.

My wife just balanced our budget. She cut herself down to 15 phone calls.

My wife just bought me a tie rack. She claims it will come in handy when she wants to hang stockings.

My wife just finished her spring cleaning. She cleaned all the springs.

My wife just got a mink coat. She gave it to herself for my birthday.

My wife just had her ears pierced—just for ventilation.

My wife just hired a handsome chauffeur. I'm a little suspicious, since we don't have a car.

My wife just took her shopping cart for a 1000-mile checkup.

My wife keeps reminding me that her allowance isn't as big as her alimony would be.

My wife knows how to make a dollar go far. She makes it go so far, I never see it again.

My wife lately changed from a hot-dish into a lukewarm dishwasher.

MY WIFE AND I

My wife leads a double life—hers and mine.

My wife left me two weeks ago. But my mother-in-law didn't.

My wife likes seductive lighting. She even put a red bulb in the refrigerator.

My wife likes to have breakfast in bed. But I have trouble getting her bed into the kitchen.

My wife loves to sign checks—on the back.

My wife must be home. The phone is still warm.

My wife must have everything to match our drapes—even our dishes.

My wife needs a TV repairman when she wants to serve a TV dinner.

My wife never opens letters addressed to me, unless they're marked 'Personal.'

My wife never wears a SMILE button. It would clash with her face.

My wife only knows two sentences: In the morning it's: "Bring home some money," and in the evening it's: "Take out the garbage!"

My wife only wants some understanding, a little appreciation and plenty of money.

My wife plays a fine game of golf. She has a beautiful backswing, except when she has a golf club in her hand.

My wife redecorated my office. She fired my cute secretary.

My wife saved all the pay envelopes, but none of the money.

My wife saves everything—like shoelaces, paper bags—everything but money.

My wife saves everything. We are the only house in town without a wastebasket.

MY WIFE AND I

My wife saves Green Stamps as if they were money and spends money as if it was Green Stamps.

My wife says I don't deserve a kind and loving wife and I agree with her. I got what I deserve.

My wife says she is pushing 115 pounds. I guess she pulls the other 20.

My wife is sometimes known as the Speaker of the House.

My wife spends all day calling her friends so they won't bother her with phone calls.

My wife spends all day in the kitchen. She doesn't do any cooking, but that's where the phone is.

My wife spends every day cleaning the house, washing dishes, shopping, cooking meals, walking the dog, mending socks, but when someone asks me if my wife works, I always say NO!

My wife started hinting she would like to see some fur. Maybe next week I'll take her to the zoo.

My wife still has wedding presents she hasn't used yet. Like a broom, iron, dusting cloth ...

My wife studies sign language. She signs for everything.

My wife sure loves checkbooks. Finished 65 already.

My wife takes her diet pills with a martini.

My wife takes me along when she goes shopping. She likes to have someone beside her to ignore.

My wife takes my shoes off when I get home and then hides them so I can't go out anymore.

My wife takes pictures Marie Antoinette style. She always cuts off the heads.

My wife talks like a revolving door.

My wife talks so much she gets a cramp in her tongue.

MY WIFE AND I

My wife told me, either I sell my golf clubs or we get a divorce. I'm going to miss her.

My wife took the money we were saving for a new car and blew it on a movie.

My wife treats my checkbook like a bestseller. She can't put it down until she's finished it.

My wife thought she would look good in something long and flowing so I pushed her into the Hudson River.

My wife uses a diet powder. She sprinkles it on her ice cream.

My wife wanted a foreign convertible, so I bought her a rickshaw.

My wife wanted a permanent gift, so I gave her a divorce.

My wife wanted something warm she could wear any place, so I got her an electric blanket with a very long cord.

My wife wanted to go overboard this Christmas, so I bought her a boat.

My wife wanted to learn how to drive. Her teacher wasn't a happy man; in fact, he cried all the time beside her.

My wife wants a divorce because I clash with the new drapes.

My wife wants a new dishwasher, but I'm not going to give her a divorce.

My wife wants a second honeymoon. She wasn't too thrilled with the first one.

My wife was spring cleaning again. My wallet is empty.

My wife watches her diet very carefully. She watches what she eats, then she eats it.

My wife went shopping to the corner market. Bought two corners.

My wife went to the butcher shop. She said she'd be back in either 20 minutes or $20, whichever came first.

My wife will always find the most expensive way to save money.

My wife will divorce me as soon as she finds a way to do it without making me happy.

My wife will never wash dishes. She has them dry-cleaned.

My wife will spend two dollars taxi fare to go to a sale, where she will cash in a coupon to get a glass vase worth ten cents.

My wife would never work a five-hour day. It takes her that long to get dressed.

My wife's back gives me trouble. She wants it covered with a new mink.

My wife's birthday is coming up. But what do you give to a woman who wants everything?

My wife's charge plates and credit cards are killing me.

My wife's diamond once belonged to a millionaire—Mr. Woolworth.

My wife's driving is improving. Last month's repair bill was less than the payment of the car.

My wife's driving is improving. Now she gets 100 miles to a ticket.

My wife's driving is improving. Now when she parks it's only a short walk to the curb.

My wife's face is so wrinkled, whenever she wears long earrings she looks like a Venetian blind.

My wife's face would be worth a fortune if she would get paid by the line.

My wife's face would not only stop a clock, it would set it back two hours.

My wife's hair is so wavy people get seasick looking at it.

My wife's hats will never go out of style. They will always look silly.

My wife's health has me worried. It's always good.

My wife's hobby is making things—like mountains out of molehills.

My wife's idea of a secret is to refuse to say who told it to her.

My wife's idea of keeping our house in order is to put me in my place.

My wife's idea of spring cleaning is emptying all the ashtrays.

My wife's kisses send me, but I'm no fool, I don't go.

My wife's laryngitis cost the phone company a fortune.

My wife's picture has to be taken with a fast camera if you want to catch her with her mouth closed.

My wife's visit to the psychiatrist was a waste of time. She spent the first forty minutes rearranging the couch.

My wife's voice gives me a pain in my ear.

Can She Cook?

All she knows about cooking is how to bring a man to a boil.

All she needs for cooking is a can opener.

Architects cover their mistakes with ivy. She uses mayonnaise.

But she is a fast cook. She serves three-minute eggs in one minute and cooks minute rice in 25 seconds.

Eating her cooking is like Russian Roulette. You never know which meal will kill you.

Even the morning paper comes to my breakfast table half burned.

Every week she buys a dozen eggs and to make sure none are cracked, she buys them scrambled.

Everything in her kitchen is electric, but her chair.

Everything she makes turns into a sandwich.

First she turned my head, then she turned my stomach.

For breakfast she serves everything instant: instant coffee, instant cream, instant pudding, instant burnt toast, but never the instant you want it.

For breakfast she serves three slices of frozen oatmeal.

Her angel food cake tastes like Hell and smells to Heaven.

Her breakfast consists of soft-boiled eggs with hard dry toast, weak coffee and a strong argument.

Her chicken a la king tastes like the chicken abdicated.

Her coffee is so dense you need two hands to dunk your doughnut.

Her coffee won't keep you awake—unless you drink it.

Her cooking is easy to identify: if it's cold it's soup, if it's hot it's beer.

Her cooking is improving. All the lumps in her mashed potatoes are the same size now.

Her cooking is improving. I used to get sick every day, now I only get sick once a week.

Her cooking is like the moon—out of this world.

Her cooking is okay as long as you don't keep it in a warm place—like your stomach.

Her cooking is so bad, if it weren't for salt and pepper I would starve.

Her cooking is so bad, she has to season her cooking with smelling salt.

MY WIFE AND I

Her cooking is so bad, the children refer to breakfast as morning sickness.

Her cooking isn't too bad, as long as you don't eat it.

Her diet is simple. If it tastes good, you have to spit it out.

Her favorite dish is a frozen peanut butter square on a stale bagel.

Her favorite meal is cold cuts with frozen corn flakes.

Her food has a way of starting out frozen and ending up burned.

Her food is either undercooked or burned.

Her food just melts in your mouth, but how often can you eat chocolate bars?

Her food kills my appetite.

Her food sometimes looks so good, I don't know, should I eat it or paint it?

Her idea of a kitchen is a place where you take food out of cans and put it on plates.

Her idea of a seven-course dinner is a roll of bologna and a six-pack.

Her TV dinners melt in your mouth. I wish she'd defrost them first.

Her lemon pie is a peach but her peach pie is a lemon.

Her meals are so bad, I have to take poison to get well.

Her meatballs are as big as grapefruits and just as sour.

Her meatballs are so big, you can either eat them or bowl with them.

Her pies don't look as bad as they taste.

Her soup is always too hot, her coffee is always too weak and her ice cream is always served too soft.

Her specialty is banana soup. I would prefer potato soup but bananas are easier to peel.

I'm not complaining, but I broke a tooth and that was with her coffee.

I'm not criticizing her cooking. But who else can burn potato salad?

I'm not saying she's a bad cook, but our garbage disposal has an ulcer.

I'm still using a piece of her first cake as a doorstop.

I asked her what we were having for dinner, and she said: "My mother!"

I bought her a cookbook but she couldn't use it. Every recipe started with: "Take a clean pan."

I bring home the bacon and she burns it.

I bring home the steak and she spoils it.

I can always tell when we have a salad dinner. I don't smell anything burning.

I caught her defrosting the stove!

I don't mind if she serves TV dinners, but re-runs?

I don't mind if she serves us mashed meatballs, but shredded goulash?

I found out the difference between vegetable soup and hash. Her vegetable soup is loose.

I hate to complain, but yesterday she tried to fry my corn flakes.

I have been eating so much frozen food, I send my compliments to our refrigerator.

I have to use a knife and fork to cut her gravy.

I just hope things never get as tough as her pot roast.

I know now what her soup needs! It needs to be thrown out!

I like when she serves a Western sandwich. It's just two slices of bread with wide open spaces in between.

MY WIFE AND I

I miss her cooking—whenever possible.

She figures one good burn deserves another.

She forgot how to make fresh orange juice.

She found a fantastic way of keeping her kitchen clean. We eat out.

She gets frostbite serving TV dinners.

She has a can opener strapped to her wrist.

She has a great cooking technique. She can make steaks taste like hot dogs.

She has me eating out of her hands. She hates to do dishes.

She has the only kitchen in the country where flies congregate to commit suicide.

She invented recycling. It's called leftovers.

She is a great cook, but her food is fattening. I walk through her kitchen and I gain five pounds.

She is a great cook. She claims, if they can freeze it, she can cook it.

She is such a bad cook, I'm the only one who likes Army food.

She is such a terrific cook that she blushes after every meal.

She is very thoughtful. She makes gravy to match my vest.

She keeps asking how many spaghetti strings I want for dinner.

She likes to cook with wine. Last night I drank a veal cutlet.

She likes to serve lukewarm brick ice cream, hard marble cake, and soft rock candy.

She made me toast every morning until she lost the recipe.

MY WIFE AND I

She makes coffee with a color the toast should be and toast with a color the coffee should be.

She makes eggnog with hard-boiled eggs.

She makes tea in a steam iron.

She needs a cookbook to make a cup of tea.

She needs two pots for her cooking—one for the food and one for the antidote.

She put a big sponge in the oven to make a sponge cake.

She put birthday candles on her fishcakes.

I wouldn't say her food is bad, but we always pray at the dinner table.

In her cooking there's something missing—the taste of food!

Is her steak tough? We had to tenderize the gravy!

My doctor advised me to drink plenty of water. I do. I drink her coffee.

My misfortune is that she looks like a cook, but isn't.

One thing about her coffee. It's not habit forming.

She always has an excuse. I bought her a foreign cookbook and now she claims she can't get any parts for the meals.

She always serves a square meal on a round dish.

She always serves blended coffee—today's and yesterday's.

She always serves coffee in a container. It gives her coffee a distinctive cardboard taste.

She baked a cake and I had to eat the whole thing. Couldn't break off a piece of it.

She bakes wonderful—on the beach!

She boiled some eggs for 20 minutes and they never got soft.

She bought a Sanka table since she never drinks coffee.

She buys frozen bread. Now she has to thaw it before she can burn the toast.

She can cook like mother and drink like father.

She can produce lukewarm ice cubes.

She does wonders with leftovers. It's the original meal I can't stand.

She doesn't know how to boil water.

She doesn't know you have to boil potatoes before you can mash them.

She even put her turkey under the sun lamp.

She needs instructions to open a cookbook.

She reads **Cooking Made Easy** while I wash the dishes.

She says it's charcoal broiled, but I say it's broiled charcoal.

She serves a dish so foreign you have to eat it with an interpreter.

She serves an X-rated turkey—very little dressing.

She serves cupcakes in paper cups.

She serves food that melts in your mouth, if you're stupid enough to put it there in the first place.

She serves hamburger incognito.

She serves our guests her home-cooked meal. But what kind of wine do you serve with heartburn?

She serves powdered orange juice, powdered eggs, powdered coffee and powdered milk. She really doesn't serve it, she blows it on you.

She serves roast beef, coffee and ice cream—all at the same temperature.

She serves soup to nuts. You get the soup and if you expect anything else, you're nuts.

MY WIFE AND I

She serves spaghetti with knots in it.

She serves the best dessert—Alka-Seltzer!

She serves TV dinners without the tinfoil. I think she's throwing away the better part.

She squeezes a can of soup to see if it's fresh.

She takes hours to shop for instant food.

She tried once to peel a raw egg.

She tried to buy some green meat for a real Irish stew.

She tried to cook in a flowerpot.

She tried to keep the pollution down by cooking with all windows closed.

She tried to make cotton candy with real cotton.

She tried to make Irish coffee with Sanka.

She tried to make pea soup by boiling Green Stamps.

She tried to open a watermelon with a plastic knife.

She tried to open an egg with a can opener.

She tried to open an egg with a hammer.

She tried to put real marble in her marble cake.

She tried to scramble a hard-boiled egg.

She even uses a tenderizer in her soup.

She wanted to buy an egg slicer for raw eggs.

She wanted to make some ice cubes, but she forgot the formula.

She was way ahead of her time. She served frozen dinners long before television.

She would like to know how long you have to cook spaghetti before it turns green.

Some people can't boil water, but she can. Only, she calls it soup.

The last time I had a hot meal was when a candle fell on my sandwich.

The last time she made some tea the tea bag got stuck in my throat.

The only thing she knows how to bake right-side up is upside-down cake.

The only way she knows how to serve steak is boiled.

There's nothing new about frozen food. I have been eating cold suppers for years.

Twice a day she opens the freezer and whatever falls out we eat.

We even make breakfast together. She makes the toast and I scrape it.

We have the best looking garbage and the most of it.

We have the only dining room table with a garbage disposal as a centerpiece.

When I complained about the food all she did was change the can opener.

When I complained her coffee was too light she put out the light to make it dark for me.

When I complained that her chicken was just skin and bones, she said, "What do you want? Feathers?"

When I once praised her beef stew, she said: "But that's your custard pie!"

When our house burned down it was the first time my food was hot.

When she cooks you get a lump in your throat, in your stomach, and in your legs.

When she gets angry she serves hot tongue and cold shoulder.

When she makes diced carrots she uses loaded dice.

MY WIFE AND I

When she misplaced her can opener she couldn't cook at all.

When she said, "Marry me and you'll always have a good cook in the house," I didn't know she meant her mother.

When she told me she couldn't cook I went out and bought her a cookbook. Then she told me she couldn't read, either!

Whenever I see croquettes on the menu, I have the feeling I missed something better yesterday.

Where there's smoke, she's cooking.

Yesterday I choked on a bone in her chocolate pudding.

Yesterday she promised me a tube-steak. It was only a hot dog.

You can ask her to cook anything as long as it is a hamburger.

You have heard of rum cake. Well, she makes a fine Pepsi Cola pie.

My Wife and I

My wife and I always flip a coin to see who does the dishes.

My wife and I are always holding hands. If we ever let go, we will kill each other.

My wife and I are always the life of the party, but it isn't always the same party.

My wife and I are both musicians. She plays the piano and I play second fiddle.

My wife and I are happily married—she is happy and I am married.

My wife and I are slowly drifting apart. Can anyone make suggestions to speed up the process?

My wife and I are very happy. She can cook and I can eat.

MY WIFE AND I

My wife and I bought a water bed and lately I found she's drifting away.

My wife and I broke up because of sickness in the family. I got sick of her.

My wife and I celebrated our tin anniversary. Twelve years of eating out of cans.

My wife and I do everything together. We even got married at the same time.

My wife and I even had an argument at the auto show. She claimed I was looking at the wrong models.

My wife and I exchanged gifts. I gave her a beaver coat and she exchanged it for a mink coat.

My wife and I got along fine for years. Then she came back.

My wife and I had a big argument about getting a dishwasher. She doesn't think I need one.

My wife and I had a 50:50 property split. She got the house and I got the mortgage.

My wife and I had words, but I never got to use mine.

My wife and I have a perfect understanding. I don't try to run her life and I don't try to run mine.

My wife and I have a very happy marriage—now and then.

My wife and I have been happily married for two years. And two out of 17 isn't bad.

My wife and I have lots of things in common—like arthritis, loose teeth, backaches...

My wife and I have reached a point where we have mutual feeling. We hate each other.

My wife and I have something in common. We're both married.

My wife and I lead a quiet life. I don't speak to her and she doesn't answer.

My wife and I like a balanced meal. Either I cook or we go out to eat.

My wife and I like the same thing. Only I like to save it and she likes to spend it.

My wife and I list our liquor bills as a medical expense since we drink to each other's health.

My wife and I often disagree, but of course, I never tell her.

My wife and I run our marriage on a 50:50 basis. I make fifty and she spends fifty.

My wife and I share everything equally. The house is in her name and all credit cards are in mine.

My wife and I sleep in different rooms, take separate vacations, have dinners apart, in fact, we do everything to keep our marriage intact.

My wife and I stuck together through thick and thin. I got thick and she got thin.

My wife and I study the market. I look at the Stock Market and she at the supermarket.

My wife and I were happily married, then she lost her job.

4

My
Friends
and
I

My friend is sure funny because ...

He acts like a puppy.

He chatters like a magpie.

He drinks like a fish.

He eats like a pig.

He gets as hungry as a bear.

He gets up with the rooster.

He goes to sleep with the chickens.

He has a spotted career.

He has his eyes on the ball.

He has his feet on the ground.

He has more crust than a pie factory.

He has the arms of an ape.

He has the eyes of a hawk.

He has the memory of an elephant.

He has the neck of a bull.

He has the shoulders of a buffalo.

He hops like a sparrow.

He is always blowing his horn.

He is as busy as a bee.

He is always coughing his head off.

He is always drunk as an owl.

He is always faithful as a dog.

He is always putting his foot down.

He is:

as blue as a nudist in Iceland.

as blue as your nose on a cold day.

as busy as a bubble dancer with a slow leak.

as busy as a person who has nothing to do.

as funny as a bee in a nudist camp.

as gentle as a lamb.

as happy as a lark.

as industrious as an ant.

as jittery as a cat up a tree.

as jumpy as a grasshopper.

as jumpy as a kangaroo.

as jumpy as a nudist who gets hot coffee spilled on his lap.

as jumpy as a tennis ball in a cement mixer.

as miserable as a centipede with bunions.

as miserable as a kleptomaniac in a locomotive factory.

as mixed up as scrambled eggs.

as nervous as a clam at low tide.

as nervous as an alligator in a handbag factory.

as nutty as a candy bar.

as nutty as a fruit cake.

as nutty as a whole peanut stand.

as relaxed as poached eggs on toast.

as relaxed as spaghetti.

as restless as a turkey in November.

as restless as a windshield wiper on a rainy day.

as restless as a butterfly.

as sensitive as a wet noodle.

as slow as a tortoise.

as sly as a fox.

as still as a mouse.

as stubborn as a mule.

as thirsty as a camel.

as vain as a peacock.

He keeps a stiff upper lip.

He keeps his eyes on the stars.

He keeps his heart in his mouth.

He keeps his nose to the grindstone.

He keeps his shoulder to the wheel.

He keeps his tongue in his cheek.

He never had a leg to stand on.

He plays like a rabbit.

He roars like a lion.

He runs like a deer.

He sleeps like a log.

He struts like a rooster.

He swims like a duck.

He thinks like a fox.

He works like a horse.

My Girl and I

I always dream about beautiful girls, but you should see the kind I get.

I always lean towards blondes, but they keep pushing me away.

I am not saying she's cockeyed, but she's the only one who can watch a tennis match without moving her head.

I am not saying she has buckteeth, but her nose looks like it's playing the piano.

I am not saying she is fat, but two more pounds and they will make her wear license plates.

I asked her father for her hand, but he said: "Take the whole girl or nothing."

I asked her if I could see her home, so she gave me a picture of it.

I asked her what she wanted for Christmas and she said that nothing was too good for her. And that's what she got—nothing!

I can read her like a book, but sometimes I forget my place.

I didn't know she was a golfer when she asked me to play around.

I don't want her when she is old and wrinkled. I want her now, when she is young and wrinkled.

I drank to her health so often, I ruined my own.

I dream of her every night. It's better than looking at her in the light.

I finally found the perfect girl. She can cook, sew, dust and repair the TV set.

I had to propose to her in the garage. I couldn't back out.

I have seen her without money but never without appetite.

I invited her over to my house for a bite. I didn't want her to bite at her house.

I knew her 40 years ago and she looked just like she looks today—old.

I like a girl to wear lipstick. I've got to have a target.

I love girls—when they let me.

I met her in the spring and was she green.

I must be getting old. All my dreams about girls are re-runs.

I never wanted to go out with girls. I wanted to stay home with them.

I only go out with good girls. I can't afford the other kind.

I really don't know much about girls—just what I've been able to pick up.

I saved my girl from being attacked last night. I controlled myself.

I think a girl should marry before she's 25. No matter how old she is.

I used to love her because of the clothes she wore, but it's all off now.

I was going around with a girl until the revolving door hit me on the head.

I'll either have to get a larger car or take out smaller girls.

I would buy her lipstick, but I don't know the size of her mouth.

I would like to have a lock of her hair. I'm stuffing a mattress.

My girl is a real athlete—always ready to play ball.

My girl is eager to meet a fellow with the same interests she has—like getting married.

My girl is showing an interest in foreign language. She just asked for a French phone.

My girl visited the psychiatrist but he couldn't get her started talking until he put a phone in her hand.

My girl uses paprika lipstick. Now her kisses burn like fire.

All About Me

I always buy from relatives. It's cheaper by the cousins.

I always celebrate Lincoln's birthday by going through his tunnel. It's not easy, since I have no car.

I always drink Mercurochrome before going to bed so I can dream in technicolor.

I always eat dessert first, because life is so uncertain.

I always eat doughnuts in this restaurant so I can look through the hole and see if anybody is stealing my hat.

I always get the same seat at the ballpark. Between the hot dog vendor and his best customer.

I always go to the auto show. I like to know what's going to knock me down next year.

I always hated school. The teacher kept asking me about things I didn't know.

I always have the last words in an argument: "Yes, dear!"

I always invite everybody to my parties. I like wall-to-wall people.

I always keep some money in my checking account. It's like money in the bank.

I always prefer a woman dentist. It's the only time I get to open my mouth to a woman.

I always thought a yard was three feet until I started cutting the grass.

I always wanted to be a dentist, but I didn't have enough pull.

I always wear sunglasses on rainy days. They protect my eyes from umbrellas.

I always wondered why babies suck their thumbs. Then I tasted baby food.

I am a home-loving guy. And that's where I would like to be right now—home loving!

I am allergic to sleeping pills. They make me drowsy.

I am crazy about winter—especially in the summertime.

I am doing my part to conserve energy. I'm taking a nap every afternoon.

I am enlarging my apartment. I'm scraping off the wallpaper.

I am for education in the schools. My kids have taught me a lot.

I am great at golf. The other day I missed a hole-in-one by four strokes.

I am happy to live in a free country where man can do as his wife pleases.

I am having trouble with my truck. The engine won't start and the payments won't stop.

I am having trouble with my typewriter. The O is upside down.

I am in favor of longer commercials on TV. It's the only chance I get to read my evening paper.

I am in perfect health. In fact, there's only one thing harder than my muscles—my arteries.

I am just waiting until the guaranteed income matches my present income after taxes and then I will retire.

I am not a YES man. When the boss says NO, I say NO.

I am not afraid of hard work. Why, I could go to sleep right beside it.

I am not going to tell you some old jokes, but I will introduce the next speaker who will.

I am not saying I carry a lot of insurance, but when I go, the company goes.

I am not saying our house is old, but we never know when the people upstairs are going to drop in on us.

I am not worried what modern children know. I'm just worried how they found out.

I am now putting all my money in taxes—the only thing sure to go up.

I am now putting some boy through college. It's the son of my TV repairman.

I am registered with an international employment agency. Now, when I'm out of work, I'm out of work all over the world.

I am so used to buying with credit cards that when I bought something for cash, I signed all the dollar bills.

I am superstitious. I won't work any week that has a Friday in it.

I am sure George Washington wasn't a sailor because anybody who stands up in a rowboat is not a sailor.

I am sure there's something wrong with my steering wheel. I missed two pedestrians already.

I am sure we met last year. I can't remember faces, but I never forget a dress.

I am the result of a mixed marriage. My father was a man and my mother was a woman.

I am thinking of giving up golf. I can't break 90 even when I cheat.

I am tired! I spent all day trying to throw my boomerang away.

I am used to public speaking. I come from a town with a party-line.

I am very famous. My name is even mentioned in one of the biggest books ever published—the telephone directory.

I am watching my drinking. I only visit bars that have mirrors.

I am well prepared for marriage. My mother gave me plenty of experience in taking out the garbage.

I am working now on something new—color radio.

I am working on big things now. I'm crossing Limburger with chlorophyll.

I asked my broker not to tell me where my money should go, and I won't tell him where he should go.

I asked the waiter what I could get for a dollar and he said: "Four quarters."

I asked the waiter where the washroom was and he told me that this was no place to do the laundry.

I ate in a place yesterday and got something special—instant indigestion.

I better go home now. I told my wife I was going out for a newspaper—and that was last night.

I blew into town yesterday. Strong wind.

I bought an automatic coffee machine, but who wants to drink automatic coffee?

I call our baby:

"Carpet" because she is always on the floor.

"Coffee" because she keeps us awake all night.

"Diploma" because she was brought home from college.

"Flannel" because she shrinks from washing.

"Grab bag" because every time you pick her up you get a surprise.

"Ivy" because she crawls all around the house.

"Teeny" because we cannot call her Martini. She isn't dry enough.

I call my bank "Tree" because it has so many branches.

I call my boss "Musketeer" because he always says I musketeer at 8 a.m.

I call my car "Baby" because it won't go anywhere without a rattle.

I call my car "Congress" because it can't pass anything.

I call my car "Flattery" because it gets me nowhere.

I call my car "Lightning" because it always goes zigzag.

I call my car "Ronzoni" because it ronzoni if you push it.

I call my child "Nose" because he's always running.

I call my dog "American Legion" because he visits every post.

I call my dog "Arctic Explorer" because he goes from pole to pole.

MY FRIENDS AND I

I call my dog "Broker" because he does all his business on the curb.

I call my dog "Bulova" because he is a watchdog.

I call my dog "Photographer" because he is always snapping people.

I call my horse "Radish" so now I can say: "Here comes my horseradish."

I call my radio "Fi" and now every night I get home, I say: "Hi Fi!"

I call my socks "Golf" because they have a hole in one.

I call my watch "River" because it doesn't run long without winding.

I call my watch "Wonder" because every time I look at it I wonder what time it is.

I call my wife "Daily"; otherwise she would get suspicious.

I call our house "Refrigerator" because it's freezing cold.

I call our toaster "Indian" because it always sends up smoke signals.

I call our turkey "Napoleon" because I always get the boney part.

I can keep a secret. It's the people I tell it to who can't.

I can lift an elephant with one hand. But I can't find an elephant with one hand.

I can make it rain any time I want to. All I have to do is to wash my car.

I can say anything I please in my house. Nobody listens anyway.

I can still remember the day when it cost more to run a car than to park it.

I can tell if it's raining by my corns. If they get wet, it's raining.

MY FRIENDS AND I

I can't understand why it's still raining. The weekend is over.

I come from a broken home. My kids have broken everything in it.

I come from a rich family. My brother is worth 5000 dollars, dead or alive.

I complimented the bank on the calendar they sent me. It's been right every month so far.

I could tell you some more jokes, but what's the use? You would only laugh at them.

I didn't even look at our baby until he was two years old. Let's face it. If you have seen one, you have seen them all.

I didn't like to go to school. At that time I couldn't read and they wouldn't let me talk.

I didn't say this restaurant was expensive, but you needed a co-signer for a ham sandwich.

I don't drink anything stronger than pop. And Pop will drink anything.

I don't have to work for a living. I could always starve.

I don't know how old I am. It keeps changing from year to year.

I don't know what to do. My heart says yes, my mind says no, and I didn't hear from my liver yet.

I don't know what to do. My piano teacher tells me to practice and my neighbors tell me to stop.

I don't know which of my two vacations I'll enjoy more this year. My own or when my boss goes on his.

I don't know who wired our house, but every time the phone rings, the lights dim.

I don't mind going to work. It's the long wait until quitting time that bothers me.

I don't mind my mother-in-law living with us. But she could have at least waited until we got married.

I don't really need a calendar. When it rains it's Sunday.

I don't speak much French—just enough to get my face slapped.

I don't spend all my money on liquor. I save some for luxuries.

I don't understand my parents. When I'm noisy they spank me and when I'm quiet, they take my temperature.

I don't want to brag, but I got a five percent loan yesterday. Five percent of what I wanted.

I don't want to say my bank account is low, but this morning they took away my calendar.

I dreamt I ate five pounds of marshmallow and in the morning my pillow was gone.

I dreamt I was eating spaghetti and then found out that the string on my pajama was missing.

I dreamt I was eating shredded wheat and when I woke up half of my mattress was gone.

I drink so much coffee, I don't snore anymore. I perk!

I dropped a lot of money in the market today. My shopping bag broke.

I dropped a quarter down the sink and had to pay the plumber $10 to get the quarter back.

I couldn't complain about the room service in this place. There wasn't any.

I finally found out why Washington was standing up in the boat. Because every time he sat down, someone handed him an oar.

I finally got a bargain in a 5 & 10 cent store. I found something that cost less than 50 cents.

I found a machine that can take apart a car in five minutes. It's called: "Locomotive."

I found a new cure for seasickness. It's called a tight collar.

I found myself in the Sahara desert in a bathing suit. There wasn't any water, but what a beach!

I found out that insanity is hereditary—you get it from your children.

I gave my kid a book as a gift and he doesn't know what to do with it. There's no place to put batteries.

I gave my secretary a week off. I've got to get some work done.

I gave up drinking. I just got sick and tired of being sick and tired.

I gave up drinking. Now I have nothing to live on but food and water.

I get plenty of exercise. Every morning I pull the ice trays out of the refrigerator.

I go to an expensive bar. They charge $24 for a Manhattan.

I got a lot of Christmas presents that were just what I wanted to exchange for what I want.

I got a watch as a wedding gift. It was the only thing in my marriage that worked.

I got four invitations to have dinner out. And they are all from my wife.

I got my hand all wet when she told me to hold my tongue.

I got one get-well card while in the hospital—from the Blue Cross.

I had a Christmas I will never forget and a New Year's I can't remember.

MY FRIENDS AND I

I had a long talk with my father about girls. And he doesn't know anything about them either.

I had a seat on the curb, but the street cleaner swept me off.

I had a 25-cent sandwich. I swallowed a quarter.

I had a 24-hour virus—a visit from my mother-in-law.

I had a White Christmas this year. When the bills came in I turned white.

I had phenomenal luck with my garden this year. Nothing came up.

I had some nice vacation. One week in Hawaii and another trying to find my luggage.

I had to buy my teen-age daughter a car. It was the only way I could get to use the phone.

I had to sell my car in order to raise money to pay the premium on the car insurance.

I hate air-conditioning. It leaves me cold.

I hate food. It always spoils my appetite.

I hate my mother-in-law. I know without her I wouldn't have my wife. And that's another reason I hate her.

I hate women who drive like they own the road and men who drive like they own the car.

I have a 50:50 arrangement with my landlord. If he doesn't ask me for the rent, I won't ask him for a receipt.

I have a fine TV set. Has only two controls—my wife and my child.

I have a mighty peculiar contract. The first clause forbids me to read any of the others.

I have a split-level house. I own half and the bank owns the other half.

I have a ten mile view from my window—looking up.

I have a two-way radio. It either plays or it doesn't.

I have all the girls eating out of my hands. I'm a waiter.

I have an unusual sunken living room. If fact, it's still sinking.

I have an unusual stock broker. He specializes in stock losses.

I have been in hot water so much, I feel like a tea bag.

I have been rich and I have been poor, and believe me, rich is better.

I have been sick on my feet for two months. I'm too strong to get sick and too weak to get well.

I have been singing since I was five. No wonder I have a sore throat.

I have been suffering from virus X. I would have had pneumonia, but I couldn't spell it.

I have been working here for four weeks and believe me, it seems like a month.

I have enough money to pay my taxes. What I need is some money to live on.

I have got nothing against water. Water is all right in its place—under bridges.

I have got one of those 90 by 10 by 15 houses. If I don't pay 90 by the 10th, I'm out on the 15th.

I have hair insurance. If all my hair falls out my policy covers my head.

I have got the only house with the cellar on the roof. They mailed me the blueprints upside down.

I have never gotten a parking ticket. I haven't been able to find a place to park.

I have never let my schooling interfere with my education.

I have never seen such waiters. When I eat alphabet soup they read over my shoulder.

I have never taken a hotel towel and I've got the silverware to prove it.

I have no trouble filing my income tax, but I have trouble paying it.

I have a wonderful insurance policy. If I bump my head they pay me a lump sum.

I have read so much about the bad effects of drinking, I gave up reading.

I have running water in my room. Too bad it never stops running.

I have seen 3-D pictures on my TV set for years: dull, dark and dated.

I have so much gold in my teeth, I have to sleep with my head in a safe.

I have some liquid assets. Two bottles of whiskey.

I have trouble with my new color TV every month. I can't make the payments.

I heard that every time a bride gets a shower, the groom gets soaked.

I heard they shot the information clerk at the bus terminal. He knew too much.

I heard you're getting a divorce. Who's the lucky man?

I heard you sing and I would call it a howling success.

I hope you live as long as your jokes.

I hung up my stockings for Christmas and sprained my back. I forgot to take them off.

I invested my money in the market—fruit and vegetable.

I joined a new Christmas Club. Every week I give my bartender one dollar and at Christmas time I get 52 free martinis.

I just bought a bottle of red ink. I'm starting my own business.

I just bought a house and on a clear day I can see the bank that holds the mortgage.

I just bought a lovely house in the suburbs. It's just two miles beyond my income.

I just bought a new color TV. Shows only two colors: black and white.

I just bought a new house, split-level. It wasn't built split-level, but the foundation settled.

I just bought a new pen. Writes under hot water.

I just found a wonderful way to improve TV dinners. I turn off the TV.

I just found out work is no good. It takes all day.

I just got back from a pleasure trip. Took my mother-in-law to the station.

I just got my car from Detroit and it cost me $10,000. They sent it airmail.

I just got some bad news from my rich uncle. He's getting better.

I just had a medical examination for my life insurance and it was renewed for thirty days.

I just heard that lipstick is poison. From now on I'll kiss my secretary through a straw.

I just heard that when a baseball player loses his eyesight, they make him an umpire.

I just realized why banks keep pestering us to save money. It might be valuable some day.

I just paid all my taxes and I'm worried. I still have some money left.

I just read a book with nothing in it—my bank book.

I just received my doctor's bill and now I know what they mean by bleeding the patient.

I just took my salary to the bank. I had to. It was too small to go by itself.

I just took two aspirin and some insect powder. I have a lousy cold.

I just want to live long enough to be as much nuisance to my children as they have been to me.

I just wish I could afford to live the way I'm living now.

I keep trying to lose weight, but it keeps finding me.

I knew I needed glasses the day I tried to dial the pencil sharpener.

I know a conceited stock broker who has a blue chip on his shoulder.

I know a politician who is so old, he doesn't run for office, he walks.

I know carrots are good for the eyes, but I nearly go blind every time I stick one in them.

I know fall is here. I just got my air-conditioner back from the repair shop.

I know he is a musician, but what does he do for a living?

I know I have an accent, but only when I talk.

I know I'm funny. When they ask me what I do, I tell them I'm a comic, so they laugh.

I know more about pigs than you'd ever dream of. I was brought up among them.

I know my capacity for drinking. The only trouble is I get drunk before I reach it.

I know my golf is improving. Yesterday I hit a ball in one.

I know these peanuts will kill my appetite. That's why I'm eating them.

I learned ice skating in six sittings.

I like a dimly lit restaurant. By the time the waiter finds the 25-cent tip, you have left.

I like antiques, but everything is so old.

I like every season. In winter I like summer and in summer I like winter.

I like my coffee black as the devil, hot as hell, pure as an angel, and sweet as love.

I like television better than the movies. It's not as far to the bathroom.

I like Thanksgiving. It's the only time I can give my mother-in-law the bird.

I like the job, it's the work I hate.

I like to eat in cafeterias. I always get good service.

I like to eat in restaurants where they have music. The music makes me forget the food and the food helps me forget the music.

I'd like to kick my friend in his teeth, but why should I improve his looks?

I like to listen, because anything I would say, I already know.

I like to run my home like a ship with me as the captain. Too bad I married an admiral.

I like to run the film of my wedding backwards. That way it has a happy ending. I walk out a free man.

I like to wear monogrammed socks so when I look under the table, I know which are my feet.

I like work. It fascinates me. I can sit and look at it for hours.

I live in a modern little apartment. So I have little room to complain.

I lost a fortune in this place. I went to bed feeling like a million dollars and woke up feeling like two cents.

I lost my entire fortune when I misplaced my wallet.

I love outdoor sports. I can sit and watch them all evening on my TV set.

I made a big mistake. At the office party I kissed the boss's secretary hello and my job goodbye.

I made a killing at the stock market. I shot my broker.

I may get to work late, but I make it up by leaving early.

I misplaced our Christmas list. Now I haven't the slightest idea who our friends are.

I never care which side my bread is buttered on. I eat both sides.

I never could get shoes that matched until I found out my feet don't match.

I never drink coffee in the morning. It keeps me awake all day.

I never drink water. I'm afraid it could be habit forming.

I never go to a film unless I've seen it before. Then I know it's good.

I never go to a restaurant anymore because I heard you shouldn't eat on an empty stomach.

I never heard a joke I didn't like.

I never liked my brother. Whenever I hit him with a hammer he would cry.

I never liked olives until someone showed me how to fix them with gin and vermouth.

I never pay any taxes. I don't have enough green to give to the Red, White and Blue.

MY FRIENDS AND I

I never really believed in ghosts until I bought a TV set.

I never remember a name, but I always forget a face.

I never was on TV but twice I was on radar on the parkway.

I never went to college because I was poor. Poor in history, poor in English, poor in arithmetic.

I often wondered why the English were tea drinkers— until I tasted their coffee.

I once bought a second-hand car and the only thing that worked right was the clock.

I once swallowed a ball, but it was all right. It was a meatball.

I only went to school on the very first day. Just to find out when our vacation began.

I ordered hot chocolate and the waiter, very busy, brought me a Hershey Bar and a match.

I ordered a vacuum cleaner by mail, but I couldn't get it out of the mailbox.

I own a great deal of Penny Stock. Too bad I bought it for three dollars.

I paid cash for everything but the battery on my new car. That I had charged.

I once painted a girl in the nude and almost froze to death.

I pay income tax like a strip-teaser. I take off as much as the law allows.

I picked up a hitchhiker the other day and broke my back. Next time I use a car.

I plan to spend a pleasant Christmas. That's about all I have left to spend.

I play golf in the low 70's. If it gets any colder I quit.

MY FRIENDS AND I

I play golf in the low 60's. Whenever I swing a golf club, I hit the ball about 60% of the time.

I play the violin exactly like Heifetz. Under the chin.

I prefer to be buried in the "No Smoking" section of the cemetery.

I put some starch in my highball and made myself a good, stiff drink.

I really don't mind the rat race, but I could do with a little more cheese.

I sacrificed everything so that my son could become a doctor, and now he tells me I have to stop smoking.

I saw a police car yesterday with an off-duty sign.

I saw my TV repairman at the ballpark. His TV set must be broken too.

I see my dentist twice a year—once for each tooth.

I see they still manufacture bathroom scales. Why? Who weighs bathrooms anymore?

I sent a letter to our local postmaster and it came back: Address unknown.

I send my mother-in-law flowers every week. She's allergic to them.

I speak eight languages. Unfortunately I speak them all at the same time.

I speak three languages: Fair French, Good German and Great Britain.

I study witchcraft to understand my mother-in-law better.

I sure hope I am sick. I hate to feel like this when I am well.

I sure love sunshine. I could sit in the sun day and night.

I think I'm going to do fine in the market this week. My broker is on vacation.

I think my landlord asks too much for the rent. Last month he asked five times.

I thought you were yourself, but now that you have come closer, I see that you are your brother.

I told my mother-in-law that my house is her house, and she sold it.

I took all my money out of the bank last night. With the bank closing at three in the afternoon it wasn't easy.

I took Dad to the golf course and listened to the happy pitter-patter of pater's putter.

I took my car to the carwash and they starched it.

I used to be a safe driver, but I gave it up. Who wants to drive a safe?

I used to be a white collar worker, but I had to quit. The collar got dirty.

I used to fish through ice, but all I got were cherries.

I used to play golf until I lost my ball—the string broke.

I visited the Washington Monument, but it doesn't look a bit like him.

I voted five times, but they can't bother me. I'm not a citizen.

I want pollution. I don't trust clean air. I like to see what I'm breathing.

I wanted to get a haircut, but they were all out of them.

I wanted to wear my vest, but when I reached for it, I noticed that somebody cut the sleeves off.

I was a beautiful child. My parents used to have me kidnapped just to see my picture in the papers.

I was a crossword puzzle boxer. I went into the ring vertically and came out horizontally.

MY FRIENDS AND I

I was a war baby. My parents took one look at me and started fighting.

I was born on the first of the month so they called me Bill.

I was born with my mother's features and my father's fixtures.

I was finally cured of that pain in the neck. My suspenders were twisted.

I was going to get some tickets for a cricket match, but who wants to match crickets?

I was going to open a loan company but my keys didn't fit.

I was my teacher's pet. She couldn't afford a dog.

I was offered a job as a baby sitter, but who wants to sit on babies?

I was so disgusted with the movie I walked out the third time I saw it.

I was so hungry I ate my shoes. I had fillet of sole, shoestring potatoes and a roast tongue.

I was so seasick I looked like my passport photo.

I was so surprised at my birth I couldn't talk for a year and a half.

I was so tough I made the teacher stay after school.

I was too poor to have treatments, so my doctor touched up my X-rays.

I was very generous this year. I gave my wife a nice check and promised to sign it next year.

I wasn't exactly a bad boy, but when I was six my parents left home.

I went back to the auto school to learn how to park, just in case I ever find a parking space.

MY FRIENDS AND I

I went down to pay my taxes and it was the first time I ever saw people fighting to be last in line.

I went to a sneak-preview and I was glad they let me sneak out.

I went to a weight watcher's restaurant and while I watched my weight someone stole my coat.

I went to an auction and got something for nodding.

I went to see the Grand Canyon and it was closed for repairs.

I will never forget my first words in the theater: "Pop corn!"

I would go on a diet, but I happen to be a poor loser.

I would like to say something funny, but I don't want to break the spell.

I would like to smother my mother-in-law in diamonds, but there must be a cheaper way.

I would like to tell a joke, but you would only laugh at me.

I would love to write my life story, but I can't remember a thing.

I wouldn't believe him if he swore he was lying.

I wouldn't say he likes to drink, but every time he bends his elbow, his mouth snaps open.

I wouldn't say my account is low, but my bank just sent me last year's calendar.

I wouldn't say the bus was crowded, but even the bus driver was standing.

I wouldn't sell this place for all the tea in China, but for cash—any time!

My ...

My ambition is to be able to afford to spend what I'm spending.

My ambition is to marry a rich girl who is too proud to let her husband work.

My apartment has running water in every room—the roof leaks.

My apartment is antique and so is my wife.

My bank account became so low, I had to give the bank back the toaster.

My bank gives out personal loans. They call them personal because when you miss a payment, do they get personal!

My bank is very careful. They send out their calendar one month at a time.

My bank just sent me a letter telling me it's the last time they will spend fifteen cents to tell me I have five cents in my account.

My barber is an authority on everything except how to cut hair properly.

My bed is so hard, I have to get up twice a night to get some rest.

My biggest vacation expense this year was my wife.

My boss cheated me out of a fortune. He wouldn't let me marry his daughter.

My boss gave me a pink slip, but what I really needed was a sweat shirt.

My boss just hired another secretary. Now he has one for each knee.

My boss offered me an interest in the business today. He said if I didn't take an interest pretty soon, he'd fire me.

My boss told me that since business is so bad, the Christmas bonus will be postponed for a year.

My boss wanted me for dinner, but I don't think I'll fit into his oven.

My boss won't let me make any personal calls at the office and my wife and daughter won't let me make my calls at home.

My brother fooled everybody. We thought he was a baby.

My brother is now studying to become a doctor. Not that he likes medicine so much, but he is crazy about double-parking.

My brother is still in the house playing duets on the piano. I finished first.

My business partner wanted an even share of the business, so we agreed—I get the ulcer and he gets the migraine.

My butcher left out the stuffing in our Thanksgiving turkey and put in the bill instead.

My car had a squeak in the back. It turned out to be my wife.

My car has only two speeds—slow and stop.

My car has something that will last a lifetime—monthly payments.

My car? I have a watch that runs better and faster.

My car is so old, it doesn't have a clock on the dashboard. It has a sundial.

My car is so small I have to pay my parking tickets in the juvenile court.

My car is so small, the radio gets only one station.

My car just came back from the laundry and all the buttons on the dashboard are missing.

MY FRIENDS AND I

My car: nobody can fix it, the garage won't park it, I can't start it, and they won't even steal it.

My cellar is so damp, when I laid a mousetrap I caught a herring.

My checking account balances perfectly. I'm overdrawn exactly what I'm short.

My child eats dry toast and washes it down with crackers.

My child has sensitive ears. He screams every time I pull them.

My children are doing so badly in school, I go to PTA meetings under an assumed name.

My credit is so bad, they won't even accept my cash.

My Dad wants to go on television. It's the only way he can get into 200 bars at the same time.

My daughter gained 180 pounds last year. Three pounds of fat and 177 pounds of husband.

My daughter has her summer all planned. She found an air-conditioned phone booth.

My daughter is in the dungarees and loafers stage. She wears dungarees and dates loafers.

My daughter is at the awkward age. She knows how to make phone calls, but not how to end them.

My daughter has been trying to run away from home for months, but every time she gets to the door, the phone rings.

My daughter is very popular. The only time the phone doesn't ring is when it's for me.

My daughter wants a flesh-colored Princess phone because it became part of her face.

My dentist got in trouble for telling jokes. He pulled too many good ones.

My dentist has no windows in his office. That's why they call him a paneless dentist.

My dentist is painless. <u>He</u> doesn't feel a thing.

My divorce was very simple. It was all a matter of give and take. I gave and she took.

My doctor advised me to give up those intimate dinners for four unless I have three more people eating with me.

My doctor, before operating on my nose and ear, asked for an arm and a leg.

My doctor couldn't be a very good doctor. All his patients are sick.

My doctor cured me of insomnia, but I still lie awake half the night thinking about my sleeplessness.

My doctor doesn't make housecalls, but if you are sick more than five days he sends you a get-well card.

My doctor finally found out what I had and relieved me of most of it.

My doctor gave me a prescription to take and believe me it was the worst tasting paper I ever ate.

My doctor gave me six months to live, but when I told him I couldn't pay his bill, he gave me another six months.

My doctor has more degrees than a thermometer.

My doctor has magic hands. Every time he touches me $50 disappears.

My doctor has the flu. Now he's getting a taste of his own medicine.

My doctor is a man who is ready to lend you a healthy hand.

My doctor is not concerned with Medicare. He never had a patient who lived to be 65.

My doctor is really nice. When he treated me for double pneumonia he charged me for one pneumonia.

My doctor is so busy, sitting in his waiting room I caught three more diseases.

My doctor is so expensive. He operated on me and charged me $300 for new parts.

My doctor is so expensive. When he told me to drink lots of liquids, I couldn't afford any.

My doctor is so mean, he keeps his stethoscope in the freezer.

My doctor is so strange. When I broke my leg he taught me how to limp.

My doctor ordered a change of scenery, so I moved my desk to the window.

My doctor said I should bathe in milk, but I couldn't get into the bottle.

My doctor said I should never sleep on an empty stomach so I always sleep on my back.

My doctor saved my life. He didn't come.

My doctor sent me a bill, marked: "Long time no fee!"

My doctor sent me a get-well card and inside was a bill for 45 cents—for the card and postage.

My doctor suggested a change of scenery so I bought new wallpaper.

My doctor, to raise my fighting spirit, handed me the bill.

My doctor told me I'm in good shape for a man of 60. Too bad I'm only 49.

My doctor told me to eat more green. Now I order my martinis with two olives.

My doctor told me to give up smoking, women and liquor. Now I'm looking for a new doctor.

My doctor told me to keep off my feet, so I took up ice skating.

My doctor told me to take something good and warm. So I took his coat.

My doctor told me to watch my food. Where I eat I have to watch my coat.

My doctor told my wife she needs some salt air. Now every morning I fan her with a salt herring.

My doctor wanted to paint my wife's throat but she couldn't decide on the color.

My doctor warned me to cut down on my drinking. So I switched from Four Roses to Three Feathers.

My doctor's phone is so busy the best way to reach him is to put an ad in the paper.

My doctor's prescription is hard to read, but his bill is nice and clear.

My doctor's reception room is always crowded, but I think people just go there to sit until they get sick.

My dog is a female watchdog. He likes to watch females.

My dog is afraid of burglars, so I put an alarm system in his dog house.

My dog was the life of the party. That gives you an idea of how dull it was.

My ear is ringing. Pardon me while I answer it.

My family was so poor we couldn't give my sister a Sweet 16 party until she was 23.

My fan club can hold a mass meeting in a telephone booth.

My father always listens to my mother. He has to. She never stops talking.

My father told me everything about the birds and the bees. He doesn't know anything about girls.

My father was killed by coffee. A 100-pound bag fell on his head.

My first date was very interesting. She was so anxious she wore a bridal gown.

My folks are sending me away to school so they won't have to help me with my homework.

My gold watch has an excellent movement—to and from the pawn shop.

My grandfather celebrated his 103rd birthday. Too bad he wasn't present. How could he be? He died when he was 40.

My grandfather is great. I call him my great grandfather.

My grandfather was an old Indian fighter. My grandma was an old Indian.

My hair will be white as long as I live and hers will be black as long as she dyes.

My hand measures nine inches. Three more inches and it would be a foot.

My history teacher was so old, she didn't teach history, she remembered it.

My house is near the river. You not only see the river, you also smell it.

My house is solid as a rock. Every time a truck goes by, it rocks.

My house is thoroughly insured. For instance, if a burglar gets hurt while robbing my house he can sue.

My house ought to be warm this winter. The painter gave it two coats.

My hubcaps keep coming off. Do you think there's too much air in the tires?

My husband grew a beard and now he kisses me through a straw.

My husband has a split personality and I hate both of them.

My husband keeps reading the wedding license searching for a loophole.

My insomnia is so bad, I can't even sleep on the job.

My landlord is always asking me to pay his rent. To pay his rent? I can't even pay my own!

My landlord is very considerate. He gives you heat in July, even if you don't ask for it.

My laundry just sent back some buttons. They lost the shirt.

My library consists of books nobody wants to borrow.

My little son likes TV better than the movies. It's not as far to the bathroom.

My marriage had its ups and downs. It started up and went straight downhill.

My marriage is a continuous process of getting used to things I hadn't expected.

My marriage was made in Heaven. So are thunder and lightning.

My mind is made up. So don't confuse me with the facts.

My money goes as far as ever. From me to my wife.

My mother is always breaking dishes, my brother is always breaking furniture, my father is always breaking an arm or a leg. I really come from a broken home.

My mother-in-law always calls me son, but she never finishes the sentence.

My mother-in-law drank so much vinegar she wound up with a pickled tongue.

My mother-in-law dropped in for a weekend. That was two years ago.

My mother-in-law feels well only when she feels ill.

My mother-in-law happens to be well informed. She can complain on any subject.

MY FRIENDS AND I

My mother-in-law has a mouth like a hamburger stand—open day and night.

My mother-in-law has been living with us for seven years. And why not? It's her house.

My mother-in-law has come to live with us. Now I have another mouth to heed.

My mother-in-law has finally reached meddle-age!

My mother-in-law hasn't spoken to me for a year. I figure the least I can do is to buy her a present to show my appreciation.

My mother-in-law is all right as mothers-in-law go, but she never does.

My mother-in-law is now in her third month of a two-day visit.

My mother-in-law is spending a month with us for a couple of days.

My mother-in-law likes to argue. She won't even eat food that agrees with her.

My mother-in-law talks so much, I get hoarse listening to her.

My neighborhood is in a residential district surrounded by private houses and apartment buildings.

My neighbors seem to like my trumpet playing. They broke my windows twice just to hear it better.

My neighbors are keeping me broke. They always buy things I can't afford.

My neighbor's furniture goes back to Louis the Fourteenth, while mine goes back to Sears on the fifteenth.

My new apartment has so many windows I get cross-pollution.

My new car is so small, the glove compartment holds only two fingers.

My new car never skids, never breaks down, never gets a flat. I only wish I could start it.

My new job is killing me. It is hard work, day after day, but I'm glad it's permanent.

My new laundry never lost a single button. Sleeves, yes, but never a button.

My new serge suit picks up everything but girls.

My new suit fits me like a glove. It covers my hands.

My new suit has a label imprinted: 100% WOOL. I'm sure the label is.

My new toaster has a built-in radio. Now we can play music while the toast burns.

My parents called me "Surrender." They took a look at me and gave up.

My parents could never afford to buy me shoes so they painted my feet black and laced my toes.

My parents never forget my birthday. I was born between the second and third payment on the TV set.

My parents were so poor, for my birthday I got a nice photograph of a birthday cake.

My parents were so poor they couldn't afford a bicycle for me, so they took off the B and gave me an icicle.

My parents were very strict. We weren't allowed to answer the phone until it rang.

My paycheck is like the tide—it comes in and goes out.

My photographs are bad but my X-rays are fantastic!

My problem is it takes me six weeks to read the book of the month.

My psychiatrist:

charges me double because I have a split personality.

cured me of drinking. He charged me so much I couldn't afford to buy liquor.

cures people by shock treatment. He bills them in advance.

has an electric vibrator installed in his couch and now picks up a fortune in loose change.

is doing so well, he had his couch upholstered four times.

is really great. He lumped all my little worries into one big complex.

is so busy, he has an upper and lower berth.

is so friendly, he lies down on the couch with you.

is so poor, he has no couch. Just a sleeping bag.

is so poor, his patients have to talk standing up.

is so poor that he can't afford a couch. He uses a cot.

is so poor, whenever he gets a patient he has to run out to rent a couch.

is so strict. He always gives me homework. I have to rush home and dream.

is so wonderful. He will always find something wrong with you.

was so henpecked, his wife always yelled whenever a patient put his feet on the couch.

My raincoat has a waterproof label. The label is waterproof, but not the coat.

My repairman refused to come and fix my air-conditioner. Claims it was too hot in my apartment.

My room has a beautiful view. If you look straight up.

My room is so cold that every time I come home and open the door, the light goes on.

My room is so small:

every time I blink I wash the windows.

every time I yawn I hit the ceiling.

every time I put a key in the lock I break a window.

every time I raise my arm I dust the furniture.

I can only fry one egg at a time.

I can't even cross my legs.

I can only brush my teeth upside down.

I can only solve crossword puzzles containing two words.

I gave the walls a second coat of paint and I couldn't get into the room.

I had to paint the furniture on the wall.

I have to go outside to change my mind.

I have to open the door when I unfold my newspaper.

I have to put the light out before I can get in.

I have to use a Dixie cup as a wash basin.

I have to use a folding toothbrush.

I have to use condensed milk.

I have wall-to-wall furniture.

I tried to gargle and blew down the ceiling.

I used a doormat as wall-to-wall carpeting.

if I dropped my toupee I'd have wall-to-wall carpeting.

it has natural air-conditioning. A broken window.

it overheats every time I use my electric toaster.

many times I used my handkerchief as a carpet.

my closet only had space for one hanger.

my dog has to wag his tail up and down.

my refrigerator is only an ice cube.

my stove is only a pilot light.

my suitcase has to be left outside.

my Venetian blind has only one slat.

the mice are hunchbacked.

when I close the door the doorknob pinches my stomach.

when I go to bed my feet stick out the window.

when I sneeze I rearrange the furniture.

when the sun comes in I have to go out.

whenever I light a cigarette the room gets over-heated.

wherever you are you can always touch all four walls.

My secretary asked me for a new pen. The old one makes too many mistakes.

My secretary can do 30 words a minute. Not typing—reading!

My secretary can take shorthand, can type 65 words a minute and can take my mind off the stock market.

My secretary can't type too well, but she can erase 50 words a minute.

My secretary had a terrible accident last week. She fell and broke her typing finger.

My secretary has a perfect attendance record. She hasn't missed a coffee break in three years.

My secretary has a new filing system. She learned it in a fish store. Anything over three days old she throws out.

My secretary is a poor speller. She even misspells P.S.

My secretary is so fat, I don't know whether to pay her by the week or by the pound.

My secretary knows how to write shorthand, but it takes her much longer.

My secretary never makes the same mistake twice. She is always able to make new ones.

My secretary quit. She caught me kissing my wife.

My secretary reminds me of my wife. Every time I whisper something in her ear, she says: "Remember you have a wife!"

My secretary says if I don't give her a raise she is going to start wearing long skirts.

My secretary spells atrociously, but others can't spell at all.

My secretary walked into my office and demanded a salary on next week's advances.

My secretary, when told to take dictation, asked me: "Where to?"

My secretary works a four-day week, but it takes her six days to do it.

My secretary wrote me a note asking for a raise, but she misspelled three words.

My shoes are so worn out, when I step on a dime I can tell if it is heads or tails.

My son has been going to a psychiatrist for years and just found out he's been deaf since birth.

My son in college likes ties with dots, suits with stripes and letters with checks in them.

My son just got a summer job. He is going to answer the phone for all his friends who go to camp.

My son refuses to study history anymore. He claims they make it faster than he can learn it.

My son shows signs of becoming an executive. Already he takes two hours for lunch.

My son started to write poetry in the hospital. I think he took a turn for the verse.

My son took an aptitude test for a job and was found best suited for retirement.

My son wanted to go places, so I bought him a chemistry set.

My son's odometer reads 85,000 miles. I'm sure he pushed the car more than that.

My summer suit is so cool, if I wear it all day I catch a cold.

My teacher has a reading problem. She couldn't read my writing.

My teacher really loved me. She kept me in her class for three years.

My tires on my car are so thin, you can almost see the air.

My trouble is that when I drink, I think; and when I think, I drink.

My TV set gave me lots of pleasure. I sold it and bought some wine.

My TV set gives me great pleasure. It keeps my wife quiet all evening.

My uncle is a stock broker. That's a blood sucker in an ivy league suit.

My uncle is a swimming instructor. He gives drowning lessons.

My uncle is in the watch business. I work and he watches.

My uncle lived to be 100. And he owes it to mushrooms. He never ate them.

My uncle took out $50,000 in life insurance. But still, it didn't do him any good. He died anyway.

My uncle used to run a Green Market. If you ate anything he sold you, that's the color you would turn.

My uncle was in the hospital for a week. It was only supposed to be one day, but he ate the food by mistake.

My watch is on the bum. My son wears it.

People

Some People

Some people are born with black eyes and some have to fight for them.

Some people are easily entertained. All you have to do is sit down and listen to them.

Some people are funny. They spend money they don't have, to buy things they don't need, to impress people they don't like.

Some people are funny. They want the front of the bus, the back of the church, and the middle of the road.

Some people are in debt because they spend what their friends think they make.

Some people are like blisters. They don't appear until all the work is done.

Some people are like blotters. They soak it all in but get it all backwards.

Some people are like pins. Useless when they lose their heads.

Some people are like rocking chairs. A lot of action, but no progress.

Some people are like taxi drivers. They go through life missing everything.

Some people are like tea bags. They don't know their own strength until they get into hot water.

Some people are like the ten-cent stamps. You don't appreciate them until they are gone.

Some people are like wheelbarrows, trailer or canoes. They need to be pushed, pulled or paddled.

Some people are now engaged in market research. They go to the supermarket, look at the prices and go home again.

Some poeple are perfect for hot weather. They leave me cold.

Some people are proud of their parking tickets. It proves they found a place to park.

Some people are saving pennies today. What else can you do with them?

Some people are so addicted to exaggeration that they can't tell the truth without lying a little.

Some people are trying to overcome the rubber shortage by writing checks that bounce.

Some people are wise and some are other-wise.

Some people aren't as anxious to get where they are going as they are to get away from where they have been.

Some people attend church three times in their lives: when they're hatched, when they're matched, and when they're dispatched.

Some people buy letter openers. I married one.

Some people can accept advice gracefully—if it doesn't interfere with their plans.

Some people can stay longer in one hour than others can in one week.

Some people can't boil water. But some do. They call it soup.

Some people can't tell a lie, others can't tell the truth, and others can't tell the difference.

Some people cause happiness wherever they go. Others, whenever they go.

Some people classify modern painting as an art disease.

Some people don't have much to say. The only trouble is that you have to wait too long to find out.

Some people drink at the fountain of knowledge, others just gargle.

Some people drink coffee and can't sleep. With me it's just the opposite. When I sleep I can't drink coffee.

Some people drive a car as if they were rehearsing for an accident.

Some people find it hard to park a car, others do it with a bang.

Some people get credit for having a nice personality when they are just proud of their teeth.

Some people get divorced while others simply get found out.

Some people get into debt trying to keep up with people who already are.

Some people get into pretty deep water trying to make a splash.

Some people get lost in thought because it is unfamiliar territory to them.

PEOPLE

Some people get on the right track and then go in the wrong direction.

Some people get seasick taking a bubble bath.

Some people get the credit for thinking, but all they do is know how to frown.

Some people grow on you, others turn out to be crop failures.

Some people have been buying so much stuff they don't need that they are starting to need stuff they can't buy.

Some people have exceptionally high standards—for other people.

Some people have heads for figures. I only have eyes for them.

Some people have more problems than an arithmetic book.

Some people have no respect for age unless it is bottled.

Some people have no taste for liquor at all. They just gulp it down.

Some people have only two faults: what they do and what they say.

Some people have social circles under their eyes.

Some people have split personalities, others lose their heads altogether.

Some people have splitting headaches, others have splitting heads.

Some people have such even tempers—always grouchy.

Some people have tact, while others tell the truth.

Some people have voices which are hard to extinguish over the telephone.

Some people have waves in their hair. I've got nothing but beach.

PEOPLE

Some people in this country have what it takes, and they work for the Internal Revenue Service.

Some people itch for success when they should be scratching for it.

Some people keep repeating the same mistakes over and over and call it experience.

Some people keep trying on shoes until the salesman has a fit.

Some people kill time by living it up

Some people kiss with their eyes closed. Too bad they also marry the same way.

Some people know a lot more when you tell them something than when you ask them something.

Some people know the price of everything and the real value of nothing.

Some people like to hear the truth no matter how flattering it is.

Some people live and learn, but some never learn.

Some people live in beautiful apartments overlooking the rent.

Some people look like they were walking around to save funeral expenses.

Some people lose their liberties by taking too many liberties.

Some people love to go to the movies while others go to the movies to love.

Some people must think I'm a revolving door. They always push me around.

Some people need three and a half cars to learn how to drive.

Some people never exaggerate. They just remember big.

PEOPLE

Some people never get interested in anything until it's none of their business.

Some people nowadays have a B.A., M.A. or Ph.D., but not many have a J.O.B.

Some people possess an amazing ability to dodge responsibility.

Some people practice what they preach, others just practice preaching.

Some people read enough to get themselves misinformed.

Some people speak from experience and others, from experience, don't.

Some people spend half their lives telling what they are going to do and the other half explaining why they didn't do it.

Some people spend so much time trying to make a killing that they forget to make a living.

Some people take cold showers with hot water.

Some people think they are busy when they're only confused.

Some people think they are worth a lot of money because they have it.

Some people think they have dynamic personalities if they occasionally explode.

Some people thirst after fame, some after love and some after money, but all thirst after salted peanuts.

Some people try to figure out the universe, while I'm trying to figure out how to start my car.

Some people try to fit a long vacation into a short bankroll.

Some people try to get something for nothing and then kick about the quality.

PEOPLE

Some people used to settle their problems over coffee and cigarettes. Now that's their problem.

Some people used to want to be rich, but now they seem satisfied just to live as if they were.

Some people watch gourmet cooking shows while eating a TV dinner.

Some people who claim they are on a diet observe it only between meals.

Some people who don't pay their taxes in due time, do time.

Some people who have half an hour to spare, usually spend it with someone who hasn't.

Some people who have things easy as pie still want it a la mode.

Some people who jump at conclusions often lose sight of the hurdle.

Some people who lose weight always seem to know where to find it.

Some people who sleep like babies never have any.

Some people who think they are dreamers are only sleepers.

Some people who think they're in the groove are just in a rut.

Some people who think they are in the swim are all wet.

Some people who think they have open minds only have holes in their heads.

Some people will believe anything if they overhear it.

Some people will do anything for money—even work!

Some people will grow up and spread cheer, others just grow up and spread.

Some people will never admit their faults. I would, if I had any.

PEOPLE

Some people will stand for anything that leaves them sitting pretty.

Some people will think the world is dirty just because they forgot to clean their glasses.

Some people with a bad cough go to the doctor, but most go to a concert.

Some people with tact have less to retract.

Some people work harder today to pay taxes than they once did to earn a living.

Some people work up steam and some only generate a fog.

Some people worry about the end of the world, but I worry only about the end of the month.

Some people you can read like a book, and some are not so easily shut up.

People I would like to meet:

an air blower.

an airplane spotter.

an ambulance stretcher.

an animal cracker.

an ant eater.

an arti-choker.

a back scratcher.

a bacon slicer.

a banana peeler.

a banana splitter.

a bargain counter.

a bedroom dresser.

a bed spreader.

a belly dancer.

a board walker.

a book worm.

a bottle opener.

a bread winner.

a brother's keeper.

a bubble dancer.

a bug killer.

a bull dozer.

a Burma shaver.

a can opener.

a card shark.

a card shuffler.

PEOPLE

a carpet sweeper.

a car shifter.

a cement mixer.

a chain smoker.

a cheap-skate.

a check bouncer.

a checkout counter.

a cheek pincher.

a chicken plucker.

a cigarette holder.

a clock puncher.

a clock watcher.

a coat hanger.

a cocktail shaker.

a cocktail mixer.

a coffee grinder.

a coffee maker.

a coin boxer.

a counter feiter.

a counter spy.

a criss crosser.

a crop duster.

a day dreamer.

a daylight saver.

a disk thrower.

a Doberman pinscher.

a door stopper.

a double crosser.

a drugstore counter.

a dumb waiter.

a dust collector.

an ear puller.

an egg beater.

an egg poacher.

an egg scrambler.

an egg timer.

an eyebrow raiser.

an eye dropper.

an eye opener.

an eye strainer.

a face lifter.

a face wrinkler.

a feather duster.

a finger tapper.

a fire cracker.

a flower sifter.

a fly catcher.

a fly swatter.

a food strainer.

a foot locker.

a gas burner.

a gas ranger.

a Geiger counter.

a ghost writer.

a glass blower.

a glass coaster.

a gold digger.

a gum wrapper.

a hair dryer.

a hair roller.

a hair teaser.

a hair waver.

a hand shaker.

a head shrinker.

an icebox raider.

an ice breaker.

a jail breaker.

a jam preserver.

a jaw breaker.

a jay walker.

a jelly roller.

a knuckle cracker.

a lawn mower.

a lawn sprinkler.

a lazy Susan.

a lemon squeezer.

a leopard spotter.

a life saver.

a lint picker.

a lint remover.

a litter bug.

a loan shark.

a lock picker.

a loud speaker.

a meat counter.

a meat freezer.

a meat grinder.

a milk dispenser.

a milk shaker.

a minute man.

a monkey's uncle.

a mother nature.

a mush roomer.

a nail biter.

a name dropper.

a napkin holder.

a needle threader.

a nit-wit.

a noise maker.

a nose dropper.

a nose picker.

a nut cracker.

an onion squeezer.

an orange shopper.

a range finder.

a record breaker.

a record changer.

a record player.

a road hog.

a room divider.

a pain killer.

a paint roller.

a party pooper.

a pencil sharpener.

a pen holder.

a penny pincher.

a peeping Tom.

a perfume sprayer.

a pick pocket.

a pillow stuffer.

a pinch hitter.

a pipe cleaner.

a pipe dreamer.

a policy holder.

a potato masher.

a potato peeler.

a pot holder.

a pressure cooker.

a safe cracker.

a salad dresser.

a salad tosser.

a salt shaker.

a Santa Claus.

a Scotch taper.

a screw driver.

a self starter.

a shock absorber.

a shoe lacer.

a shop lifter.

a shoulder guard.

a silent butler.

a sky diver.

a sky scraper.

a slave driver.

a snow blower.

a socks stretcher.

a steam roller.

a steeple chaser.

a sugar bowler.

a television tuner.

a time saver.

a tongue depressor.

a tongue sharpener.

a tooth picker.

a towel wringer.

a town crier.

a trouble maker.

a trouble shooter.

a tuna fisher.

a turkey stuffer.

a two timer.

a type writer.

an Uncle Sam.

a vacuum cleaner.

a wall scraper.

a weight watcher.

a West Pointer.

a wind breaker.

a window shopper.

a windshield wiper.

a wise cracker.

Funny Definitions About People:

Accountant:

A desk jockey.

A figurehead.

A person who feels good when things start looking black again.

A person who is hired to tell you, you didn't make as much money as you did.

A person who is paid to make figures lie.

A person who uses your books to figure his profit.

Actor:

A man who, if you aren't talking about him, he isn't listening.

A man who is trained to keep a large group of people from coughing.

A man who plays when he works and works when he plays.

A man who tries to be everything but himself.

A show off.

The only ham that can't be cured.

Ad Libber:

A person who stays up all night to memorize spontaneous jokes.

Admiral:

A general at sea.

Adolescence:

The age between pigtails and cocktails.

The age between puberty and adultery.

The age when a boy stops collecting stamps and starts playing post office.

The age when a child tries to bring up his parents.

The age when a girl's voice changes from NO to YES.

The age when boys begin to notice that girls notice boys who notice girls.

The age when children begin to question the answers.

The time when children feel that their parents should be told the facts of life.

The wonderful age when boys discover girls and girls discover they have been discovered.

Adolescent:

A youngster who acts like a baby when you don't treat him like an adult.

A youngster who is old enough to dress himself, if he could just remember where he dropped his clothes.

A youngster who is old enough to get up in the morning, but not quite sure how to progress from there.

Adult: A person who has stopped growing at both ends and has started growing in the middle.

Agent:

A person who hates actors because they take 90 percent of his salary.

A pickpocket with a license.

Aggressive Feline: Pushy cat.

Agriculturist: A farmer with a station wagon.

Airline Stewardess:

A plane Jane.

A tipless waitress.

Ambassador:

A politician who is given a job abroad in order to get him out of the country.

An honest person sent abroad to lie for the commonwealth.

American:

A person who:

acts like a Texan when he gets to Europe.

after eating a typical American dinner of chow mein and blintzes, has some Swiss cheese, English tea, Spanish rice and Portuguese sardines, and after having some pizza, goes to his Volkswagen to drive to another town to see a French movie.

after emptying an ashtray, may manage to look as if he's just finished house cleaning.

always remembers his wife's age but forgets her birthday.

always remembers his wife's birthday. It's the day after she reminds him of it.

as soon as he can afford a Plymouth, goes out and buys a Cadillac.

attends church three times in his life. When hatched, when matched and when dispatched.

boils water to make hot tea, adds ice to make it cold, adds sugar to make it sweet and adds lemon to make it sour.

buys a chair that vibrates and a car that doesn't.

buys a lifetime supply of aspirin and uses it up in two weeks.

buys Italian shoes, French toilet water, Continental suits, Persian rugs, Dutch cheese, a German Dachshund, Turkish cigarettes, gets an English cottage with French windows and a French poodle, and wants to be recognized as a true American.

calls himself a bachelor until he gets married. Then you should hear what he calls himself.

can always tell what kind of a time he has at a party by the look on his wife's face.

can say anything he pleases in his own home. His wife and children never listen anyway.

celebrates July 4th by getting into a Volvo, driving to the beach on Arabian gas, rolling out a Hong Kong blanket and listening to a Sony while smoking Cuban cigars, drinking Scotch whiskey, or eating Danish pastry or Dutch chocolate.

content years ago to wait three or four days for a stage coach. Now complains if he misses one section of the revolving door.

demands better roads, bigger schools and lower taxes.

does know, but never remembers the words to the "Star-Spangled Banner."

doesn't know what he wants and kills himself trying to get it.

doesn't mind spending money as long as he knows it isn't going for taxes.

drinks to forget the woman who is driving him to drink.

drives a bank-financed car over a bond-financed highway on credit-card gas, to open a charge account at a department store, so he can fill a savings-and-loan financed home with installment-purchased furniture.

drives last year's car, wears this year's clothes and spends next year's salary.

first buys a home and then buys a car to get away from it.

gets acquainted with a neighbor by meeting him down in Florida.

gets lots of credit. How else could he buy a new car every year?

gets together with other people to talk about the hard times over an $18 steak.

goes into a bar for an eye-opener and comes out blind.

goes on a vacation in a hurry to slow down.

goes through the change of life when his child is born. It changes his life.

hammers on the radiator for more steam, while dressing to go skiing.

has a Japanese gardener, a Chinese houseboy, a French maid, a German cook, an Irish chauffeur, a Swedish housekeeper, an American secretary and a Mexican divorce.

has acquired a huge vocabulary by marrying one.

has both feet on the ground and both hands up in the air.

has burned his fingers trying to grab the Toast of the Town.

has enough money to last a lifetime, unless he buys something.

has enough money to pay taxes. What is needed now is some money to live on.

has learned to work faster, relax less, spend more and die quicker.

has more food to eat than any person in any other country, and more diets to keep him from eating.

has more time-saving devices and less time than any other person in the world.

has no trouble filing an income tax report. Only has trouble paying it.

has the highest standard of living. Too bad he cannot afford it.

is deeply interested in the problem of space, especially parking and closet.

is looking for home atmosphere in a hotel and hotel service at home.

is proud of his right to say what he pleases, and often wishes he had the courage to do so.

is 39 around the chest, 40 around the waist, 96 around the golf course, 132 around the bowling alley, seldom around the house when needed and a nuisance all the time.

is too proud to steal, too proud to beg and too poor to pay cash. That's why he gets credit all over.

isn't afraid to holler at the President, but he is always polite to a policeman.

just wishes he could afford to live the way he is living now.

keeps insisting for the latest edition of the evening paper and then only reads the comics.

knows exactly when to take out the garbage—as soon as his wife tells him.

knows the complete lineup of all the baseball teams, but only the first line of the "Star-Spangled Banner."

knows when and where the Pilgrims landed, but has no idea why.

learns arithmetic to be able to keep the baseball scores.

likes to relax in a tub. He enjoys it so much that sometimes he even fills it with water.

lives in a topsy-turvy country where people eat upside-down cake, doors go round in circles and everybody has an inside outhouse.

loses his balance when he goes shopping.

orders a new car three months before it comes out and then buys Christmas presents on December 24th.

pays so much insurance to take care of the future that he is starving to death in the present.

rushes around all day to save time which he will waste at night.

sips Brazilian coffee from an English cup while sitting on Danish furniture after coming home in a German car from a Swedish movie and then writes to a Congressman with a Japanese ball point pen demanding to know why so much gold is leaving the United States.

smokes English tobacco, wears Italian shoes, often eats Chinese food, or French fries and English muffins, takes a foreign car to strange places with borrowed luggage to eat Hungarian goulash and Irish stew.

spends a lot of money for a garage, and then parks the car outside.

spends half of his money on coffee to keep awake and the other half on sleeping pills to sleep at night.

spends more time with the TV set than with the spouse.

uses instant coffee to dawdle away an hour.

would like to have a car that will last as long as the payments.

would like to have a five course 500-calorie dinner.

would like to have a good five-second commercial.

would like to have a litter basket big enough to hold the old car.

would like to have a nine-to-five coffee break.

would like to have a pill that will make a person enjoy raking leaves more than playing golf.

would like to have a power mower that can be operated from an air-conditioned room.

would like to have a President who knows what this country needs.

would like to have a quick-drying cement that sets before kids can walk on it.

would like to have a spot remover that removes spots left by other spot removers.

would like to have a supermarket cart with four wheels all pointing in the same direction.

would like to have a vending machine that honors credit cards.

would like to have an ashtray that looks like one.

would like to have fewer people explaining what this country really needs.

would like to have fewer wise guys and more wise people.

would like to have less permanent waves and more permanent wives.

would like to have less soiled conversation and more soil conservation.

would like to have more free speech that's worth hearing.

would like to have more whittlers and fewer chiselers.

yells for speed laws that will stop fast driving and then won't buy a car if it can't go 100 miles an hour.

yells for the government to balance the budget and borrows five dollars till payday.

yells with the neighbors, fights with the employees, disagrees with the minority groups, fights with the family and can't understand why the United Nations don't get along with each other.

Angry Father: Mad dad.

Anesthetist: Gas man.

Archeologist: Someone whose career lies in ruins.

Architect: A man who covers his mistakes with ivy.

Astronaut:

A cloud hopper.

A person who is able to play golf on the moon.

A spaceman who finds a place in the sun by reaching for the moon.

A whirled traveler.

Astronomer:

A person who looks at the moon when not in love.

A person whose business is always looking up.

A night watchman.

Auctioneer:

A person who picks out your wallet with a hammer.

A person who sells nothing for something to a buyer who is looking for something for nothing.

Autograph Collector: A big name hunter.

Average Person:

Any person who thinks he is above average.

Any person you see everywhere but in the mirror.

What we all think we are not.

Babies: Little rivets in the bond of matrimony.

Baby:

A child loved by mother.

An alimentary canal with a loud voice on one end and no responsibility on the other.

Last year's pleasure with lungs.

Mama's little yelper.

Newly wet.

The only person who can have a toothache without having any teeth.

Baby Calf: New moo.

Baby Carriage: Last year's fun on wheels.

Baby Hair: Beginner's lock.

Baby Nursery: Wet set.

Baby Quadruplets: Four crying out loud.

Baby Sitter:

A teenager who behaves like a grown-up, while grown-ups behave like teenagers.

A teenager who gets two dollars an hour to eat five dollars worth of food.

A person who gets paid hush money.

A person who gets 75 cents an hour to wear out the TV picture tube.

A person you pay to watch TV while the children cry themselves to sleep.

A person you sometimes hire to join your kids watching TV.

A yelper helper.

Bachelor:

A man who:

always aims to squeeze.

always went on double dates in college.

avoids bride-eyed women.

believes in life, liberty and the happiness of pursuit.

believes in wine, women and so-long.

believes that one can live as cheaply as two.

can forget his mistakes.

can get into bed from either side.

can go fishing anytime, until he gets hooked.

can have a girl on his knee without having her on his hands.

can leave his socks and wallet lying around the house.

can open his wallet without turning his head.

PEOPLE

can take a nap on top of the bedspread.

can tell his symptoms to his doctor without having his wife interrupt.

can use his home phone whenever he wants.

can't be spouse-broken.

can't stand the strain of a wife.

cheated some woman out of a divorce.

comes to work every morning from a different direction.

doesn't get around to marrying. He just gets around.

doesn't have to leave the party when he starts having a good time.

expects to marry just as soon as he finds a girl who loves him as much as he loves himself.

failed to embrace his opportunities.

gets tangled up with a lot of women in order to avoid getting tied down to one.

is a free male.

is a permanent temptation.

is a rolling stone that gathers no boss.

is allergic to wedding cakes.

is crazy to get married and knows it.

is foot-loose and family-free.

is foot-loose and fiancée-free.

is known as a dame dropper.

is looking for a date with no apron attached.

is lucky in love.

is never miss-taken.

is not missing anything in life except a few buttons on his shirt.

is smart enough not to go on a hayride with a grass widow.

knew when to stop.

knows all the ankles.

knows how to hold a woman's hand so that she doesn't get a grip on him.

knows if he has a steady girl on the string he may wind up on a leash.

knows more about women than men. That's why he is a bachelor.

knows more than one willing girl.

leans toward a woman but not far enough to fall.

likes his girl friend just the way she is—single!

looks, but does not leap.

lost the opportunity of making a woman miserable.

makes mistakes but not in front of a preacher.

never chases a woman he couldn't outrun.

never knows whom the next kiss is coming from.

never lied to his wife.

never makes the same mistake once.

never met a girl he couldn't live without.

never Mrs. anything.

never needs altarations.

never says: "I'll give you a ring tomorrow!"

plays the game of love and manages to retain his amateur standing.

prefers ripe tomatoes with little dressing.

refuses to fight.

takes a girl out until she wants to get married.

thinks he is a thing of beauty and a boy forever.

travels fastest in a parked car.

tries to avoid the issue.

usually has his hands full trying to loosen a woman's grip.

wakes up in the morning with all of the blankets.

wants a girl on his arm, but not on his hands.

washes only one set of dishes.

when a girl asks him for a diamond ring, he turns stone-deaf.

when he opens the window in his apartment, more dust blows out than in.

would rather mend his socks than his ways.

won't take 'yes' for an answer.

would rather change girls than change their names.

would rather cook his own goose.

would rather have a woman on his mind than on his neck.

would rather wash his own socks than dry his wife's dishes.

wouldn't change his quarter for a better half.

Bachelor Girl: A girl who is still looking for a bachelor.

Backseat Driver:

A driver who drives a driver.

One who never runs out of gas.

Back-Slapper: A person who hopes you'll cough up something.

Baker:

A person who has his fingers in many pies.

A person who rolls in dough.

Ballerina:

A dancer who toes her way around.

A girl gone crazy with her feet.

Band Leader:

A person who makes you dance to his tune.

A person who must face the music.

Banjo Player: A musician who has easy picking.

Bank Teller: A person who makes piles of money.

Barber:

A brilliant conversationalist who occasionally shaves and cuts hair.

A person known as a cliptomaniac.

A person known as a head gardener.

A person who gets paid to get in your hair.

A person to whom you have to take off your hat.

Bargain Shopper:

A person who will buy anything she thinks the store is losing money on.

Bathing Beauty:

A girl who has a lovely profile all the way down.

A girl who wears nothing to speak of, but plenty to talk about.

A girl worth wading for.

A sand witch.

Beautiful Bride: One who is well-groomed at a wedding.

Beautiful Girl: A slick chick.

Beauty:

A girl who often runs her face into a handsome figure.

The best substitute for brains.

Best Man:

An usher who made good.

The one who doesn't get the bride.

Bigamist:

A man who:

adds one and has two to carry.

believes variety is the spice of wife.

carries two pictures of wives in his otherwise empty wallet.

doesn't know when he's got enough.

doesn't know when to leave bad enough alone.

got the wrong number.

has taken one too many.

leads a double wife.

leads two wives.

learns too late that two rites make a wrong.

likes to keep two himself.

loves not too wisely, but too well.

makes a second mistake before correcting the first.

makes the same mistake twice.

marries a beautiful woman and a cook.

marries twice in a wifetime.

thinks the plural of spouse is spice.

washes twice as many dishes after meals.

Bill Collector:

Backdoor pounder.

The person who doesn't forget you when you have no money.

The person who never forgets your address.

Blabbermouth: A person who doesn't know what to say and then goes ahead and says it.

Bore:

A person who:

always has lots of time to spare.

as guests go, you wish he would.

can talk long enough to put you to sleep, but loud enough to keep you awake.

deprives you of your privacy without providing you with company.

gets offended when others talk while he's interrupting.

has a one-track mind.

has a supply of talk that exceeds the demand.

has nothing to say but you have to listen a long time to find out.

has to hold your lapel to hold your attention.

holds a cocktail glass in one hand and your lapel in the other.

if you ask him what time it is, will start to tell you how to make a watch.

is always arriving and never leaving.

is always giving you twice as many details as you want to hear.

is harder to get rid of than a summer cold.

is here today and here tomorrow.

is known as the still life of the party.

is so full of sayings that should go without saying.

is very oft-spoken.

keeps you from being lonely and makes you wish you were.

knows a few words, but uses them at great length.

knows a million ways to start a conversation and none to end one.

knows the same stories you do.

lights up the room when he leaves.

lost the art of conversation but not the power of speech.

never goes without saying.

never runs out of conversation—just listeners.

never seems to have a previous engagement.

never tries to make a long story short.

not only holds a conversation, he strangles it.

opens his mouth and puts his feet in.

says a thousand things, but never says goodbye.

sees that your company leaves at a reasonable hour.

syndicates the conversation.

takes his time taking your time.

tells you it's a small world and makes you wish it were bigger.

thinks he is cultured because he can bore you on any subject.

uses his mouth to talk while you use yours to yawn.

wants to talk when you want to read and wants to read when you want to talk.

will eat with his fingers and talk with his fork.

will never talk about other people, only about himself.

won't listen when you talk about yourself.

would rather change his friends than his subject.

whenever there's a dull in the conversation, you'll find him in the middle of it.

whose shortcoming is his long-staying.

whose stories always have a happy ending. Everybody is happy when they end.

you like better the more you see him less.

Boss:

A person who comes in early to see who comes in late.

A person who will raise the roof before he will raise your salary.

Boxer:

A person who always hurts the one he gloves.

A person who always puts his best fist forward.

A person who makes money hand over fist.

A person who often doesn't know which side his head is battered on.

Boy:

A lot of dirt with noise.

A lot of noise with dirt.

A noise covered with smudges.

A person who gets his hands dirty washing his face.

Brat:

A child who always displays his pest manners.

A child who, when he gets what he wants, doesn't want it.

A spoiled child who is always too fresh.

Bride:

A girl who begins a new life.

A girl who goes from lipstick to broomstick.

A girl who turns into a wife.

A miss who suddenly becomes a Mrs.

Bridegroom: A man who spends a lot of money on a new suit that no one notices.

Broker:

A person who runs your fortune into a shoestring.

A person who wants to tie you up in stocks and bonds.

What you become when you play the stock market.

Bus Driver: The only man who can tell a lady where to get off.

Businessman:

A man who is bald and fat because he comes out on top after pushing his way to the front.

A man who spends time making money and then spends money killing time.

Busybody:

A person who burns a scandal at both ends.

A person who is never busier than when engaging in something that's none of his business.

Butcher:

A person who is always ready to pick a bone with you.

A person who makes both ends meat.

A person who's usually long on waits and short on weight.

A steak holder.

An awkward person whose hands are always in his weigh.

The only person who will admit he has no brains.

The person least likely to put on extra weight.

Caddy:

A little cad.

An employee who is always left holding the bag.

One of those little things that counts.

Candidate:

A person who runs for office while claiming he will win in a walk.

A person who stands for what he thinks the people will fall for.

A politician who quotes from public opinion polls until defeated, and then mumbles something about the ignorance of the masses.

Capitalist:

A person who continues to spend less than his income.

A person who gathers a fortune he doesn't need, to leave to people who don't deserve it.

Career Woman: A person who is more interested in the shape of her future than the future of her shape.

Careful Driver:

A motorist on the way to court to pay a speeding ticket.

A motorist who can sneak his car out of the garage without being caught by his wife.

A motorist who just saw a driver ahead of him getting a ticket.

Careless Driver: A fender bender.

Cashier:

A person who counts in this world.

A person who is in a paying business.

A quick change artist.

Celebrity:

An actor with a publicity agent.

An employed actor.

One who works all his life in order to be well-known and then goes through backstreets wearing dark glasses to avoid being recognized.

One whose name is in everything but in the telephone book.

PEOPLE

Censor:

A person who specializes in cutting remarks.

A person who sticks his no's into other people's business.

Census Taker: A person who goes from house to house increasing the population.

Census Taker in China: Chinese checkers.

Character:

A jerk with personality.

What a man is in the dark.

What one is called if one doesn't have any.

What you have left when you've lost everything you can lose.

Charge Account Addict: Civilian casualty.

Chatterbox:

A telephone booth.

Any person who talks like a revolving door.

Chauffeur: A person smart enough to drive a car and clever enough not to own one.

Chef: A person with a big enough vocabulary to give the soup a different name every day.

Chess Master: Concentration champ.

Child: A thing that stands halfway between an adult and the TV screen.

Childish Game: One at which your wife beats you.

Children:

Small people who aren't permitted to act as their parents did at that age.

The little things that tell.

Unreasonable facsimiles.

Child's Bicycle: A tot rod.

Chiropractor:

A doctor who gets paid for what I get slapped for.

A doctor who is called a slipped disk jockey.

A doctor who kneads patients.

A doctor whose fees are all back pay.

Columnist:

A person who gives you the lowdown on the higher ups.

A person who knows tomorrow why the things he predicted yesterday didn't happen today.

A person who tells people who go to bed at a decent hour the doings of those who don't.

Comedian:

A person with a fun-track mind.

A person who doesn't think he is funny but hopes other people will.

A person who has a gift of gag.

A person who makes dough out of corn.

A person who originates old jokes.

Commuter:

A human yo-yo.

A person who goes to the city every day to make enough money to sleep in the country.

A person who pays short visits to his home and office.

A man who shaves and takes a train, and then rides back to shave again.

A man who spends his life in riding to and from his wife.

Comparison Shopper: Counter spy.

Composer: A bad pianist with good memory.

Conductor: A person who isn't afraid to face the music.

Conservative:

> A person who doesn't think that anything should be done for the first time.

> A person who is too cowardly to fight and too fat to run.

> A person who is slightly center of the center.

Consultant: A person who is called in at the last minute to share the blame.

Consumer: A person who hits the ceiling every time prices do.

Convict: The only person who likes to be stopped in the middle of a sentence.

Cook: A pan-handler.

Coordinator: One who transforms unorganized confusion into regimental chaos.

Coward:

> One who, in a perilous emergency, thinks with his legs.

> Yellow fellow.

Creditor: A person who has a better memory than a debtor.

Critic:

> One who finds a little bad in the best things.

> A person who goes places and boos things.

Counterfeiter:

> A person who gets into trouble by following a good example.

A person who has to make good money in order to stay in business.

A person who makes money without advertising.

Counter-Irritant: A person who looks at everything and buys nothing.

Counter Spy: Department store detective.

Cynic:

A person who believes the world is neither round nor flat, but crooked.

A person who knows the price of everything and the value of nothing.

A person who, when he smells flowers, looks around for the coffin.

Daydreamer:

A person who goes through life having a wonderful time spending money he hasn't got.

A person who has a good foundation for building castles in the air.

A person who has done most of his dreaming while he's awake.

Defendant: A person who should always have a lawyer unless he has a friend on the jury.

Defender: Part of a car.

Dentist:

A person who:

always bores you to tears.

always tries to pull a fast one.

dents things.

finds work for his own teeth by taking out those of others.

gets paid for boring you.

gives you a pain that drives you to extraction.

grinds out a day's work.

is a bridge builder.

is always getting on your nerve.

is always looking down in the mouth.

is called a 2th doc.

lives from hand to mouth.

nobody wants to see more than twice a year.

only pulls the tooth, the whole tooth and nothing but the tooth.

repairs broken bridges.

runs a filling station.

thinks a tooth is stronger than a friction.

tickles your ivories.

will give you the drill of your life.

Diplomat:

A person who:

always knows what to talk about, but doesn't always talk about what he knows.

always tries to settle problems created by other diplomats.

can always make himself misunderstood.

can bring home the bacon without spilling the beans.

can convince his wife not to hide her nice body under a floor-length sable.

can convince his wife to show off her new coat in a bus rather than in a taxi.

can juggle a hot potato long enough for it to become a cold issue.

can keep his shirt on while getting something off his chest.

can look happy when he has unexpected dinner guests.

can make his wife believe she will look fat in a mink coat.

can make nothing sound like something.

can put his best foot forward when he doesn't have a leg to stand on.

can put his foot down without stepping on someone's toes.

can say the nastiest things in the nicest way.

can tell a man he's open-minded when he means he has a hole in his head.

can tell you to go to hell so tactfully that you look forward to the trip.

comes right out and says what he thinks when he agrees with you.

divides his time between running for office and running for cover.

fills the air with speeches and vice versa.

has a straightforward way of dodging issues.

has great faith in his own patience.

has to watch his appease and accuse.

knows how far to go before he goes too far.

lets you do all the talking while he gets what he wants.

never tells a woman how nice she looks in a gown. He tells her how nice the gown looks on her.

praises married life while staying single.

puts his cards on the table but still has some up each sleeve.

straddles an issue whenever he isn't dodging one.

thinks twice before saying nothing.

when asked his favorite color replies: "Plaid!"

when he surprises a lady in the bathtub will say: "Pardon me, sir!"

will approach every question with an open mouth.

will lay down your life for his country.

will refuse to answer any question on the ground it might eliminate him.

Disc Jockey: A person who lives on spins and needles.

Discharged Record Spinner: A slipped disc jockey.

District Attorney: Someone awful but lawful.

Diva: A woman swimmer.

Diver:

A person who always throws himself into his work.

A person who jumps headfirst into the water.

Doctor:

A person familiar with many tongues.

A person who enjoys poor health.

A person who is ready to lend you a healthing hand.

A man who is required by law to know all about women.

A person who suffers from good health—in his community.

A person whom you see for regular checkups to prevent a permanent checkout.

A person you stick your tongue out to.

Druggist:

A person who used to sell drugs.

A person who wishes everybody ill.

A soda jerk with a diploma.

Drugstore Clerk: A fizzician.

Dumb Cherub: Stupid cupid.

Economist:

A person who:

denies himself a necessity today to buy a luxury tomorrow.

has a plan to do something with somebody else's money.

has all the answers to last year's questions.

is a big noise in his place of business, but just a little squeak at home.

is in business to change other people's business.

is uncertain about the future and hazy about the present.

knows all the answers, but doesn't understand the questions.

knows how to throw money he doesn't have after money he never had.

knows more about money than people who have it.

knows tomorrow why things he said yesterday didn't happen today.

talks in millions and borrows carfare to go home.

tells you how to spend your money without getting any fun out of it.

tells you that in days of rising prices, a dollar saved is 80 cents lost.

tells you what to do with your money after you've done something else with it.

tells you what's wrong with the world and makes you think it's your fault.

when he doesn't know the answer, changes the subject.

Editor:

A literary barber.

A person who keeps things out of the paper.

A person with a little desk and a big wastebasket.

Efficiency Expert:

A person who is smart enough to tell you how to run your business, but too smart to start his own.

A person who spends six years in college learning how to look busy while watching you work.

Egoist:

A person of low taste, more interested in himself than in you.

A person who is his own best friend.

A person who talks about himself when you want to talk about yourself.

A person who's always me-deep in conversation.

An I-dropper.

Electrician:

A person who wires for money.

A switch doctor.

Elevator Operator:

A human yo-yo.

A person who has his ups and downs.

English Horn Teacher: Tudor tooter tutor.

Eskimos:

People who:

after a few months of work call it a day.

are called God's frozen people.

are sitting on top of the world.

have to undress with an ice pick.

make pies.

move in the best arctic circles.

Executive:

A person who:

can make quick decisions and is sometimes right.

can take two hours for lunch without hindering the production.

can't take more than three hours for lunch, because it would cut his cocktail hour.

decides quickly and gets somebody else to do the job.

delegates all the responsibility, shifts all the blame and takes all the credit.

dreams up an idea, has an assistant who says it can't be done, and a secretary who does it.

follows the work schedule to a tee.

goes around with a worried look on his assistant's face.

has an answer to everything and a solution to nothing.

is a big gun that hasn't been fired yet.

is always annoying the hired help by asking them to do something.

knows something about everything.

likes the feel of a good desk under his feet.

makes independent decisions without being fired.

starts on the bottom and works everybody.

takes two hours on the phone to explain why he can't see you for 10 minutes.

talks to visitors so others can get some work done.

travels from his air-conditioned office in an air-conditioned car to his air-conditioned club to take a steam bath.

Expert:

A person who:

can take something you already knew and make it sound confusing.

cuts so many corners, everybody's going around in circles.

has a difficulty for every solution.

has a good reason for guessing wrong.

is an expert as long as he guesses right.

is from out of town.

is just beginning to understand how little he knows about the subject.

is known as a small-talk expert. If there's nothing to be said he will say it.

is seldom in doubt but often in error.

knows a lot about very little and keeps on learning more and more about less and less, until he finally knows all about nothing.

knows all the answers if you ask the right questions.

knows more and more about less and less.

makes his mistakes quietly.

waits to make up a four for a foursome before going through a revolving door.

walks in his sleep so he can get his rest and exercise at the same time.

Explorer: A person who gets enough material for a lecture.

Exporter: A person who used to work as a porter.

Exterminator:

A person who is always dressed to kill.

The person who comes once a month to feed the mice.

Eye Doctor: Winker tinker.

Family man:

A man who doesn't get a chance to read the Sunday paper until Monday night.

A man who replaces the money in his wallet with snapshots of the wife and kids.

Farmer:

A person who:

can make plenty of money if he sells his farm to a golf club.

is always outstanding in his field.

tips his hat every time he passes a tomato.

works from daybreak till backbreak.

Father:

A kin I love to touch.

A man for whom the monthly bill tolls.

A man in the family who is neither seen nor heard.

A man who buys the frills, pays the bills, and signs the wills.

A man who is wired for cash.

Financial Genius: A man who can earn money faster than his wife can spend it.

Fireman:

A person who doesn't have to be told to go to blazes.

A person who never takes his eyes off the hose.

Forger:

A person who gives a check a bad name.

A person who is always ready to write a wrong.

A person who tries to make a name for himself, but picks the wrong one.

Friend:

A person who goes around saying nice things about you behind your back.

A person who has the same enemies you have.

A person who is in your corner when you are cornered.

A person who will eventually borrow money from you.

A person who will love you forever in spite of your success.

A person with whom you dare to be yourself.

Gambler:

A person who knows that money can be lost in more ways than won.

A person who never knows where the next deal is coming from.

A person who picks his own pocket.

A person who worries when his bookies don't balance.

Genius:

A crackpot until he hits the jackpot.

A person who has the ability to avoid work by doing it right the first time.

A man who can make money faster than his wife can spend it.

A person who can do almost anything except make a living.

A person who can rewrap a new shirt and not have any pins left over.

Some other woman's husband.

Gentleman:

A man who:

> doesn't get fresh until the second evening.

> gives a lady his standing room when he leaves the bus.

> helps a woman across the street even if she doesn't need help.

holds the door open for his wife while she carries in a load of groceries.

is a wolf with patience.

is a worn-out wolf.

is polite to you even when he has no favor to ask.

steadies the stepladder for his wife while she paints the kitchen ceiling.

will step on his cigarette so it won't burn the carpet.

wouldn't strike a lady with his hat on.

Gentleman Farmer:

A farmer who dresses his scarecrow in a tuxedo.

A man who never raises anything but his hat.

Girl:

A person who is always something of three things: hungry, thirsty, or both.

A person who is fanatical about fashion but is not wrapped up in it.

A person who will scream at a mouse but smile at a wolf.

A young lady with bride ideas.

A young woman whose maiden aim is to change her maiden name.

Something a man looks damn silly dancing without.

The skin he loves to clutch.

Usually a vision in the evening and a sight in the morning.

What every young man should know.

What women over 40 call each other.

Girl Mechanic: Tool pigeon.

Girl Putting on Makeup: Baiting the trap.

Girl Watchers: Peer group.

Girl's Suitor Doorbell ringer.

Golfer:

> A person who hits and tells.
>
> A person who yells "FORE," takes six and puts down five.

Grandmother:

> A baby sitter who doesn't hang around the refrigerator.
>
> An old lady who comes to your house, spoils the children and then goes home.
>
> An old lady who keeps your mother from spanking you.
>
> The forgotten baby sitter.

Housewife: A woman who, when it comes to housework, likes to do nothing better.

Husband:

> A man who:
>
>> feels his pocket every time he passes a mailbox.
>>
>> gave up privileges he never knew he had.
>>
>> is spouse-broken.
>>
>> just listens when he talks to his wife on the telephone.
>>
>> knows that what a woman says is never done.
>>
>> lost his liberty in pursuit of happiness.
>>
>> made a wrong turn in lovers' lane.
>>
>> pushed his luck too far.

thinks there ought to be a law to out-law in-laws.

wears his pants in the house—under his apron.

A bachelor whose luck finally failed him.

A domestic animal.

A grouch a woman often nurses.

A man of few words.

A person whose chief function is to pay bills.

A woman's companion and paymate.

An average man who gets married before he has sense enough not to.

What is left over of a sweetheart after the nerve is removed.

Hypochondriac:

A person who:

can read a doctor's handwriting.

can't leave being well enough alone.

claims he strained his back lifting $15 worth of groceries.

enjoys poor health and complains when feeling better.

feels bad when he feels good because he's afraid he will feel worse when he feels better.

finding a feather in his bed, thought he had the chicken pox.

goes to a cocktail party and stirs his drink with a thermometer.

goes to a drive-in movie in an ambulance.

goes to medical school to study to be a patient.

has a sick sense.

has a three-room medicine chest.

hates to hear how well he looks.

insists on being buried next to a doctor.

is an impatient patient.

is happy being miserable.

is so afraid of germs he won't even lick a stamp.
Puts it on with a safety pin.

is terribly unhappy when he is happy.

likes to speak ill of himself.

takes overseas shots before going to a foreign
movie.

wants to have his ache and treat it too.

Hypocrite:

A person who:

can't tell the truth without lying.

hands his paycheck to his wife with a smile on
his face.

looks before he weeps.

pays his taxes with a smile.

says grace over a meal prepared with a can
opener.

says he likes doing the dishes.

Infant:

A disturber of the peace.

A household object that gets you down in the
daytime and up at night.

Innocent Bystander:

A person so simple-minded he doesn't know enough
to get out of the way.

The person who always gets hurt.

Interior Decorator:

A person who does things to your house he wouldn't dream of doing to his own.

A refined house painter.

Janitor:

A floor-flusher.

A person known by the temperature he keeps.

A person who starts on the bottom and warms up.

A person who would rather sleep than heat.

The last person to learn that there has been a drop in temperature.

Judge:

A lawyer who knew a politician.

A man in a trying position.

A referee between two lawyers.

Junk Dealer:

A person who is always down in the dumps.

A person who makes cash from trash.

Juvenile Delinquent:

A minor who is a major problem.

Children acting like their parents.

Other people's children.

Landlord: A person who aims to lease.

Lawyer:

A person who:

helps you get what is coming to him.

is known as a fee-loader.

is willing to go to court and spend your last cent to prove he is right.

keeps you out of jail by putting you in the poorhouse.

will read a 10,000 word document and call it a brief.

is his best when doing his worst.

Lazy Butcher: A meat loafer.

Man:

A person who:

is the only animal that drinks when not thirsty and makes love all season.

wishes he were as wise as he thinks his wife thinks he is.

Mother-in-Law:

A guest you never invited.

A matrimonial kin that gets under your skin.

A person who frequently goes too far by remaining too near.

A puzzle full of crosswords.

A spy in your house.

A talkie that has come to stay.

A woman who comes into the house voice first.

A woman who gives orders in your house.

A woman who has a hot temper and a cold shoulder.

A woman who is never outspoken.

A woman who seldom goes without saying.

A woman who tells you what to eat and when.

Another figure of speech, relatively speaking.

The only crank that can't be turned.

What you inherit free of charge when you marry your wife.

Motorist:

A driver who:

after seeing a wreck, drives carefully for a few blocks.

forgot that he used to be a pedestrian.

has either auto insurance or accidents.

knows that the car to watch is the car behind the car in front of him.

not only takes good care of his car, but also keeps pedestrians in good running condition.

pays in the long run.

the more he steps on the gas, the less shoe leather he wears out.

Mountain Climber:

A person who:

should always foot the hills.

should never lose himself in his work.

wants to take another peak.

Movie Star:

A woman who:

conceals her age but reveals her figure.

divorces her husband when she needs publicity.

goes to parties only to show off her latest mink and her latest husband.

is usually in mink condition.

never knows where her next husband is coming from.

Musician:

A band aid.

A person who earns his living by playing around.

A person who helps many singers with his playing. He drowns them out.

A person who plays when working and works when playing.

Neighbor:

A person who:

advises you what to buy so he can borrow it later.

buys things he can afford to show off to people who can't appreciate them.

can watch you taking it easy without thinking you're just lazy.

comes to your door and exchanges a little dirt for a little sugar.

is always trying to borrow things.

is always doing something you can't afford.

is here today and gone to borrow.

knows more about your affairs than you do.

listens to your conversation through the wall.

used to drop in for a call but now calls in for a drop.

wonders when your loud party will end.

New Yorker:

A group of people who feel rich because they charge each other too much.

A man who gets acquainted with his neighbor by meeting him down in Florida.

A man who has never seen the Statue of Liberty or a parking place.

A man who will all but break his neck to save ten minutes he will waste anyway.

Oculist:

A doctor you go to see when you can't see.

A person with an eye for business.

Old Timer:

A person who remembers when:

a baby was an addition and not a deduction.

a bureau was a piece of furniture.

a caller rang the doorbell instead of blowing the horn.

a car salesman said 500 he meant the price and not the horsepower.

a coffee break was your lunch hour.

a couple used to go driving in the park instead of parking in the drive.

a day's work took a day and not a week.

a dishwasher had to be married and not bought.

a dollar was worth fifty cents.

a hero meant a person, not a sandwich.

a man did his own withholding on his take-home pay.

a summer vacation was one day at the county fair.

a wife put food in cans instead of taking it out.

PEOPLE

a wife's meals were carefully thought out rather than thawed out.

a woman married a man for his money instead of divorcing him for it.

air pollution was corned beef and cabbage.

air was clean and sex was dirty.

an allergy was just an itch and all you did was scratch it.

baby sitters were called mothers.

campers were people and not trucks.

coffee was a grind and paying for it was not.

dancing was done with the feet.

doctors used to smoke and kids didn't.

eight-forty was the time the play started and not the price of the ticket.

five-and-ten stood for cents, and not for dollars.

girls stayed home because they had nothing to wear.

he made the last payment on his house.

he mailed a penny postcard for two cents.

health foods were whatever your mother said you'd better eat or else.

it took a whole week to spend a week's pay.

people aimed to get to Heaven instead of the moon.

people stopped spending when they ran out of money.

people worried about the national debt.

rockets were part of a fireworks celebration.

scientists taught that everything that goes up must come down.

setting the world on fire was merely a figure of speech.

sex education was learning to kiss without bumping noses.

the biggest danger a housewife faced in the kitchen was a burn, not frostbite.

the only garbage problem was getting your husband to put it out.

the wonder drugs of the day were castor oil and camphor.

the younger generation used to go to bed before the adults.

things in dime stores were a dime.

we had trees on the streets instead of parking meters.

we sat down at the table and counted our blessings instead of calories.

we used to kill time by working.

wives rocked the cradle instead of the boat.

women wore nightcaps instead of drinking them.

you were only broke the day before payday.

your coffee break came with the meal.

Optimist:

A person who:

asks his wife to help him with the supper dishes.

believes everything he reads on book jackets.

believes the thinning out of his hair is only a temporary matter.

built a small swimming pool right next to where Noah was building his ark.

buys a box of grass seed and a new lawn mower the same day.

buys a lifetime pen and expects it to last at least a month.

counts his change while running for a bus.

doesn't give a darn what happens as long as it doesn't happen to him.

expects change from a taxi driver.

fastens the seat belt before starting the car on a cold morning.

figures when his shoes wear out he'll be back on his feet.

gets married at 80 and then buys a house near a school.

gets married on Independence Day.

goes down with a fishing pole when the basement is flooded.

goes into a hotel without luggage and asks to have a check cashed.

goes into a restaurant without any money and hopes to pay with the pearls he will find in the oysters.

goes to a summer resort a friend has recommended.

goes to the supermarket with $10 and takes a cart.

hurries because he thinks his wife is waiting.

is a happy-chondriac.

is a hope addict.

is always able to laugh at your trouble.

is an anti-skeptic.

is happy to feel rosy.

is planning what to do with the money left over after taxes.

keeps his motor running while his wife pops in to buy a new hat.

keeps the motor running while waiting for his wife to get dressed.

lets his creditors do his worrying.

lights a match before asking for a cigarette.

looks for pork in a can of pork and beans.

looks forward to enjoying the scenery on a detour.

maintains that everything is right when it is wrong.

makes $100 a week and marries a girl crazy about children.

makes the best of it when he gets the worst of it.

manufactures hair restorer and gives out free combs with every bottle.

marries his secretary and thinks he will continue dictating to her.

never had much experience in anything.

opens a hat shop before the mirrors are delivered.

plays gin rummy with his wife.

says he's only going to watch the start of the late, late show.

sees the bright side of the other person's misfortune.

sees an opportunity in every calamity. A pessimist sees a calamity in every opportunity.

sees only the down payment.

sends a package by parcel post and marks it rush.

sends his income tax in an unstamped envelope.

sets aside two hours to do his income tax return.

sits in the tenth row and winks at the chorus girl.

spends his last dollar to buy a new wallet.

takes a bath when he finds himself in hot water.

takes a camera along when going fishing.

takes a frying pan along on a fishing trip.

tells you to cheer up when things are going his way.

thinks a fly is looking for a way out.

thinks a woman will hang up the phone just because she said goodbye.

thinks a $20,000 house can be built for 20,000 dollars.

thinks he has already had all his bad breaks.

thinks he has no bad habits.

thinks he will never do anything stupid again.

thinks humorists will eventually run out of definitions of an optimist.

thinks marriage will end all troubles.

thinks the woman he is going to marry is better than the one he has just divorced.

went to court to find out when the marriage license expires.

when he falls in the water, considers himself in the swim.

will leave his door unlocked hoping his wife will walk out on him.

wipes off his glasses before starting to eat a grapefruit.

Paratrooper:

A dropout.

A person who climbs down trees he never climbed up.

A person who has to pull strings to stay in his job.

Parking Lot Attendant: Professional fender bender.

Pawnbroker:

A loaner.

A person for whom it's never too late to lend.

A person you have to put up with.

A person you have to see after you've done business with your stock broker.

A person who hopes you will see him at your earliest inconvenience.

A person who lives on the flat of the land.

A person who takes great interest in serving the poor.

A time keeper.

Pedestrian:

A case of survival of the fittest.

A girl who doesn't neck.

A married man who owns a car.

A motorist with three good tires.

A person who always has that run down feeling.

A person who always has the right of wait.

A person who counted on his wife to put some gas in the car.

A person who doesn't know where his next car is coming from.

A person who falls by the wayside.

A person who has failed to keep up the payments on the car.

A person who has finally found a parking space.

A person who has just bought a used car.

A person who has learned it doesn't pay to go straight.

A person who has the right of way when he is in an ambulance.

A person who has two cars and a wife and a son.

A person who ignored his wife when she asked for a second car.

A person who is always found in front of cars.

A person who is here today and run over tomorrow.

A person who is looking for the place he parked his car.

A person who is safe only when he is riding.

A person who lives longer these days provided he is rushed to a hospital.

A person who needs automobile insurance.

A person who parked his car far away.

A person who should be seen and not hurt.

A person who thought his battery would last another day.

A person who, when he crosses a street, hopes to get the brakes.

A person whose son is home from college.

A person whose wife beat him to the garage.

A person whose wife has gone off with the car.

A street walking object invisible to the motorist.

One who leaps before he looks.

The most approachable person in the world.

The raw material for an accident.

The vanishing American.

Peeping Tom:

A night watchman.

A peek freak.

A window fan.

A wolf, window shopping.

People:

Something like boats, they toot the loudest when they are in a fog.

The only thing wrong with the world.

Pessimist:

A man who:

always does better today than he expects to do tomorrow.

always finds something to worry about once he puts his mind to it.

believes that life is neither worth living nor leaving.

blows out the candles to see how dark it is.

buys more than one lifetime pen.

complains about the noise when opportunity knocks.

constantly keeps his bad breaks relined.

crosses his fingers when he says: "Good Morning!"

crosses the street and his fingers at the same time.

expects nothing on a silver platter except tarnish.

expects to find bad news in a fortune cookie.

feels bad when he feels good for fear that he'll feel worse when he feels better.

forgets to laugh, while an optimist laughs to forget.

has financed an optimist.

has lost his heart and has to depend on his liver.

hesitates to pick a flower out of fear it might turn out to be poison ivy.

is a disappointed optimist.

is a misfortune teller.

is a reformed optimist.

is afraid the optimist is right.

is always putting his alarm around you.

is always seeing the germs in the milk of human kindness.

is happy when he is wrong.

is never happy unless he is miserable.

is seasick during the entire voyage of life.

lives with an optimist.

looks both ways before crossing a one-way street.

never develops eyestrain looking at the bright side of things.

sees a cloud in every silver lining.

sees only the hole in the doughnut.

sizes himself up and gets angry about it.

thinks if he reaches down to pick a four-leaf clover he will probably be bitten by a snake.

thinks no trouble is as bad as no trouble.

thinks that everybody is as nasty as himself, and hates them for it.

when he has the choice of two evils, chooses both.

would ask in a Chinese restaurant for a misfortune cookie.

would commit suicide if he could do it without killing himself.

Pharmacist: A person in a white coat who stands behind a soda fountain selling two-dollar watches.

Philanthropist: A person who gives away what he should give back.

Philatelist: An eccentric person who pays more for used stamps than for new ones.

Philosopher:

A person who always knows what to do until it happens to him.

A person who can look at an empty glass with a smile.

A person who doesn't care if both parties to the argument are wrong.

A person who knows that nothing ages a woman as fast as trying to stay young.

Photographer:

A person who can make an ugly girl pretty as a picture.

A person who takes your picture and makes you pay for it.

Pickpocket:

A person who:

believes that every crowd has a silver lining.

is a garment worker.

is a person of abstraction.

is a trouser browser.

is a wallet collector.

is always finding things before people lose them.

never knows where his next steal is coming from.

will always extend a helping hand.

will always pick his way through a crowd.

Plumber:

A drain surgeon.

A person who gets paid for sleeping under other people's sinks.

A person who makes a living when the spirit is willing but the flush is weak.

Plumber Apprenticeship: Basic draining.

Plumber's Assistant: Drainee Trainee.

Podiatrist:

A doctor who bills the foot.

A doctor who is always down at the heel.

A doctor who knows his bunions.

A doctor who makes money hand over foot.

Politician:

A person who:

always saddles a question.

can give you his complete attention without hearing a word you say.

can sit on a fence and keep both ears to the ground.

can talk for an hour without mentioning what he was talking about.

changes sides more often than a windshield wiper.

doesn't mean what he says and doesn't say what he means.

faces every question with an open mouth.

finds out which way the crowd is going, then jumps in front and carries the flag.

gets into the public eye by getting in the public's hair.

has his hands in your pocket, his mouth in your ear, and his faith in your patience.

hits the ceiling as soon as he takes the floor.

if he can't say anything bad about his opponent, won't say anything at all.

is always for the people but against the public.

is known as a dealer in promises.

is so busy he has no time to be honest.

knows how to say nothing, just doesn't always know when.

needs three hats. One he tosses in the ring, one he talks through and one he eats.

plays both sides against the taxpayer.

says: "Nice to see you again," even if he has never seen you before.

shakes your hand before election and pulls your leg afterwards.

takes money from the rich and votes from the poor, and promises both sides protection from each other.

tells you who to vote for.

usually belongs to the opposite party.

will stand for anything that will leave him sitting pretty.

Producer: A person who gives the public what they want and hopes they want it.

Psychiatrist:

A person who:

doesn't have to worry as long as others do.

goes to a burlesque show to watch the audience.

goes to a movie and understands the picture.

if he didn't have a medical degree, would be considered just plain nosey.

makes money using other people's heads.

makes you crazy, then makes you pay $25 to prove it.

tells people how to stand on their own feet while reclining on couches.

when a pretty girl enters a crowded room, looks at everybody else.

will listen to you as long as you don't make sense.

A couch coach.

A doctor who can't stand the sight of blood.

A doctor with a couch.

A head coach.

A mental detective.

A mental peeping Tom.

A mental pickpocket.

A mind sweeper.

A nut cracker.

The last person you talk to before you start talking to yourself.

Radio Announcer:

A person who talks until you have a headache, then tries to sell you something to relieve it.

A person on the ether who should be under it.

Radio Comedian: A network nitwit.

Relative:

An inherited critic.

A person who comes to dinner who isn't a friend.

Scientist:

A person who calls ordinary things by such long names that you think he's talking about something else.

A man who can rave about nylons when they are empty.

A person who is always trying to prolong life so we can have time to pay for all the gadgets he invents.

A person who works himself to death so that he will be remembered after he is dead.

Specialist:

A doctor who has patients trained to become ill only during office hours.

A person who concentrates more and more on less and less.

Stewardess:

A flying waitress.

A tipless waitress.

Plane girl.

A girl who has to smile coast to coast.

Taxi Driver:

A person who:

> drives away customers.
>
> goes through life just missing everything.
>
> is always picking up strangers.
>
> runs into many interesting people.

Teenagers:

People who express a burning drive to be different by dressing exactly alike.

Youngsters who regard home as a drive-in where Pop pays for the hamburgers.

Toastmaster:

> An expert on making toast.

> A person who introduces a person who needs no introduction.

> A person who eats meals he doesn't like and tells stories he doesn't remember to people who have heard it before.

Tourist: A person who travels thousands of miles to get a picture of himself standing by the car.

Trombonist:

> A man who is always blowing his own horn.

> A man who succeeds by letting things slide.

Veterinarian:

> A doctor who makes horse calls.

> A doctor who treats his patients like dogs.

Well-Bred Man: A man who can insult another person in public and make it sound like brilliant conversation.

Wife:

> A woman who:

>> can dish it out but can't cook.

>> dresses to kill and cooks the same way.

>> generally speaking, is generally speaking.

>> has a made-up face, serves heated-up dinners, charges-up bills, and has a fed-up husband.

>> is a dish-jockey.

>> is a former sweetheart.

>> is a husband's bitter half.

>> is a sparring partner.

>> is a thing of beauty and a jaw forever.

>> is a walkie-talkie.

is most attached to a man.

is something a man can't get along with or without.

is the contrary sex.

learned how to tie a beau.

learns that it can be just as hard to find a man after marriage as before.

like an umpire, never believes her husband is safe when he's out.

plays bridge, tennis, golf, and dumb.

reaches for a chair when answering the telephone.

sits up with you when you are sick and puts up with you when you are not.

sticks with her husband through all the troubles he would never have had if he hadn't married her in the first place.

wants a roof over her head and a husband under her thumb.

when you hear somebody in the kitchen tidying up, it's her mother.

would rather mend your ways than your socks.

Window Shopper:

A store gazer.

An eye browser.

Woman:

A person who:

can skin a wolf and get a mink.

can stay longer on the phone than on a diet.

dresses for men's eyes and for women's eyebrows.

goes to a football game to look at mink coats.

is a girl with wrinkles.

is a member of the speaker sex.

is a member of the unfair sex.

is a member of the weeper sex.

is always thinking it takes two to keep a secret.

is God's second mistake.

is the female of the speeches.

is the kind of problem men like to wrestle with.

is the sex that always concerns itself with why, when and wear.

is the so-called tender gender.

needs shoes larger inside than outside.

never knows her worst faults until she quarrels with her best friend.

remains in the twenties between teen-age and middle-age.

sometimes gets so tired she can hardly keep her mouth open.

will spend $20 on a slip and be annoyed if it shows.

Woman Driver:

A driver who believes that one bad turn deserves another.

A driver who gets caught in a traffic jam that wouldn't have happened if she wasn't there.

A driver who is always taking a turn for the worse.

A fender bender.

Woman Golfer: Reckless driver.

PEOPLE

Woman Gossip: A gab bag.

Woman's Dress Shop: A wear-house.

Woman's Fashion: Those things that go in one year and out the other.

Woman's Handbag: Steamer trunk.

Woman's Intuition: A suspicion that turns out to be true.

Woman's Purse: A velvet-lined junkyard.

Woman's Tea: A place where females go to giggle, gab, gobble, and git.

Woman's Tears: The most efficient water power in the world.

Woman's Tennis Match: Volley of the Dolls.

Woman's Tongue: Something that does not go without saying.